SUCCESSFUL
LEADERS
OF THE
BIBLE

Also by Katara Washington Patton

Successful Moms of the Bible

Successful Women of the Bible

SUCCESSFUL LEADERS OF THE BIBLE

KATARA WASHINGTON PATTON

New York Boston Nashville

FaithWords
Hachette Book Group
1290 Avenue of the Americas, New York, NY 10104
faithwords.com
twitter.com/faithwords

First Edition: January 2017

FaithWords is a division of Hachette Book Group, Inc. The FaithWords name and logo are trademarks of Hachette Book Group, Inc.

The publisher is not responsible for websites (or their content) that are not owned by the publisher.

Library of Congress Cataloging-in-Publication Data

Names: Patton, Katara Washington, author.
Title: Successful leaders of the Bible / Katara Washington Patton.
Description: first [edition]. | New York : Faith Words, 2017.
Identifiers: LCCN 2016044184| ISBN 9781455538874 (trade pbk.) | ISBN 9781455538881 (ebook)
Subjects: LCSH: Bible—Biography. | Success—Biblical teaching. | Leadership—Biblical teaching.
Classification: LCC BS571 .P29 2017 | DDC 220.9/2—dc23 LC record available at https://lccn.loc.gov/2016044184

ISBNs: 978-1-4555-3887-4 (trade pbk.), 978-1-4555-3888-1 (ebook)

Printed in the United States of America

LSC-C

10 9 8 7 6 5 4 3 2

This book is dedicated to all of the wonderful leaders and mentors (too many to begin to name) I've had the opportunity to observe. I've learned a great deal from watching you!

Contents

SUCCESSFUL
LEADERS
OF THE
BIBLE

Introduction

Leader can be a broad description for anyone who influences others. Leaders include the CEO developing and carrying out a vision for an organization, a mother who manages her household, a pastor leading a congregation, and the Girl Scout leader sharing life skills with a troop of impressionable young girls. Leaders are teachers, administrators, students, doctors, lawyers, entertainers, and so on. Leaders are those who make a difference in someone else's life (whether that's a large group or just one person). If you look closely, you will see a leader within. We are all called to be leaders in one way or another, influencing, inspiring, and shaping one another's lives.

But how do we lead well? How do we serve God by serving God's people well? Again, the Bible has the answers. Our road map for life gives us a multitude of case studies on successful leadership. From what to do well to what not to do, we can find it in God's Word.

Explore with me ten of the Bible's successful leaders—how they met their goals and lived out their God-given mission to serve people. We will see they all had ups and downs and trials and tribulations, and throughout this book we will use their examples to find our own path toward successful leadership.

God has not left us without help. God has given us all we need to live successfully. It's in God's Word—awaiting our discovery. Let's use the Bible—and our imagination—to study the actions of those labeled as successful leaders so that we might find mentors and guides through biblical history to pattern our lives from and follow. We do not walk alone. We have a cloud of witnesses who have gone before us, who have encountered similar situations in a different time frame. Let's use their wisdom to propel us into success.

Joseph

> Successful leaders grow and develop through adverse circumstances as they pursue their God-given dreams.

You intended to harm me, but God intended it all for good. He brought me to this position so I could save the lives of many people.

(Genesis 50:20, NLT)

Every human being has a dream at one point or another. Kids dream about growing up and being teachers, firefighters, or police officers. Teens dream about being independent and free from their parents. Adults dream about creating a good life for their families. Successful leadership starts off with a dream, whether big or small—a desire to be better, a desire to do better, or a desire to help someone else.

Yet life will show us that dreams don't often happen as we play them out in our minds; they grow and morph and change. And the mark of a successful leader is that he or she can grow and change with those dreams even when they seem faraway and out of reach. The way a person handles setbacks and challenges can be an accurate predictor of his or her ability to be a successful leader. We can all do good work under great conditions, with the support of our team, the love of our family, and encouragement from friends. But what happens when things go sideways or when you're the only one believing in your dream? Do you give up and bury the dream? Do you rehearse the issues, deciding the circumstances at hand are too overwhelming to overcome? A successful leader keeps moving forward, no matter how gloomy the forecast appears. He is always looking for new opportunities and paths to get to the goal. She uses adverse conditions to regroup and double up her efforts to forge ahead. True leaders have an inner determination to follow their dreams and vision no matter what happens. Even when their dreams seem far off, they hold on to their goals.

Look at Joseph's life. He exemplifies perseverance. He was given a dream at a very young age, as many of us are too, but he had no idea what he would go through to reach that goal. Yet his setbacks did not deter him; they propelled him to grow into a successful leader.

When we first meet Joseph in Genesis 37, he was his father's favorite son. Joseph was born to Jacob, also named Israel, in his late age (Genesis 37:3) and with the woman he loved the most (Rachel). Joseph was born into love—he was wanted and cherished and nurtured (oh, for every child to have this privilege). Joseph was the golden child, the one who garnered sweet memories as his father gazed upon him. Joseph was the one who received the best handpicked gifts from his father. If he lived today, he'd be the best-dressed child in class. He'd be the one with the expensive education. With all the privileges afforded to him, one would think Joseph was destined to be a leader. But even the privileged have to be developed into leaders. Your ability may seem natural—and it may be even God-given—but it will need to be developed. And like it or not, our best lessons and opportunities for growth come from our setbacks. How you handle adversity will determine your propensity for success.

The Dream

Very early on in the account of Joseph in Genesis, we learn that this favorite son had been given a dream—or vision—by God at a very young age. Joseph dreamed that he and his brothers were gathering bundles of wheat, and his bundle stood upright while his brothers' wheat bowed to his. He had another dream confirming his status as a leader: he dreamed the sun and moon and stars bowed to him (Genesis 37:6–9.) Joseph was destined to lead. Yet his immaturity seeped through; he still needed to be developed into a successful leader.

When he was given a dream that his brothers would bow down to him, Joseph didn't seem to stop even for a second to consider how this news would make his brothers, who were older, feel. He was so focused on his dream, he hadn't taken the time to consider its impact on anyone else. I hear him, excited to share the good news revealed to him. I hear his immaturity speaking loud and clear, assuming everyone will eagerly jump on board just because he has a vision.

Hey, brothers. I got some exciting news to share with you. I had a dream the other night, and I want to tell

you about it. You all were in my dream too. Yes, Reu-
ben, Simeon, Levi, Judah, Issachar, Zebulun, Dan,
Naphtali, Gad, and Asher—my dream included all of
my big brothers. I was in the center. And y'all? Y'all
were right there with me, bowing down to me. It's like
the grain we gather. Just one bundle stands out while
the others fall down around it. In my dream, my wheat
stood straight up while the others lay down. That's us—
can't y'all see it?

But wait, if you don't get that dream, I even had
another dream—it's like confirmation. Let me tell
y'all about that. But this time, instead of grain, God
gave me a vision with the stars, moon, and sun—all
the beautiful things God created. All of these beauti-
ful creations of God bowed to me—me, Joseph. It was
amazing. Can't y'all see this vision—the stars, sun, and
moon all acknowledging little ole me? It was a great
dream! I'm going to be great and in the center. Y'all
will be there with me—supporting my greatness. Isn't
God good? God is going to bless our family. I can't wait
to see my dreams come true... can't y'all, big brothers?

Now just imagine what the older brothers were
thinking as they listened to Joseph pour out his
vision:

What, the youngest will be the one we bow to? Huh?

Really? He's got to be crazy if he thinks we're going to follow him. Just because he's Dad's favorite doesn't mean he's ours. He thinks we are going to sing backup in his band. That's so not going to happen, little Joseph. We are not going to sit back and let you be in the center. Nope. It's not our mission in life to support you. Only in your dreams will we bow to you, young man. You are not our sun, stars, or moon.

I can imagine those older brothers sharing the same expressions I've seen in meetings when the over-eager leader has attended a conference and is excited to share all of the new findings and the new improvements she is bringing to the organization. Every single employee is probably thinking: *And who's going to do that?* (Newsflash, dreamcaster: already overworked workers are not always eager to hear about the dream you see so clearly in front of your nose; all they hear from your vision is more work!) The leader casting the vision is probably right on point, like Joseph was. But what about the timing of this vision-casting session? What about the audience Joseph is sharing his goals with? A mature leader takes her audience and the timing into consideration when sharing goals.

Did Joseph really have to open his big mouth and share this with his brothers? Why didn't he consider how they might feel about his dreams? Everyone we meet does not need to hear how great we are, how wonderful we will become, all the promises we have stored up just for us. Really? Who wants to hear about you all of the time anyway? And even when the vision includes the group or family or organization we lead, a successful leader always takes into account what his listeners will hear; she cares enough to think of others first before proceeding with messages. Everything does not have to be delivered right now and in a manner that is insensitive or untimely. At the end of the month when all reports are due is probably not the best time to call a meeting about all of your new ideas, which you just so happened to conjure while you got to get away and enjoy a conference in a sunny offsite location. A leader considers the audience and the timing before he opens his mouth and shares the dream.

Leadership Takes More than a Dream or Vision

And while Joseph's dream was from God, Joseph may have been misguided as to what it really meant.

God can give us visions and dreams, but rarely do we fully understand how these things will come to pass or even what they mean when they are first given to us. We'd mess them up or graciously decline the offer if God laid out all of his plans for us in the beginning!

With God-given dreams, we only see a portion of what God is calling us to do, and if we are not careful, we, like Joseph, can allow our human and partial vision to proclaim something that isn't really about God but about us. As a young boy, the leader Joseph couldn't see—or didn't care to see—how his father's favoritism coupled with his dreams impacted his relationship with those he would eventually lead. He was excited. He was enthusiastic, yet he had no idea what it would take for his vision to come to bear.

After sharing his dream of leading his brothers, Joseph is, unbeknownst to him, registered for the most aggressive leadership training program around—the ups and downs of life. Fueled by jealousy, Joseph's brothers sell the favored son and dreamer to traveling merchants, who resell him into slavery to an Egyptian officer (Genesis 37:28–36). Through serving in a foreign country as a slave, Joseph learns more than one can gather from an MBA at a top business school.

Joseph, in essence, has an internship with Potiphar—the Egyptian official he assists.

So Joseph, the one who dreams of others bowing to him, was forced into service in a foreign land. The irony of leadership is that it's not about being in charge but really about serving. Joseph undergoes real-time training, first as a slave and then as a trusted assistant. And, in the midst of his circumstances, his character emerges. Yes, Joseph was destined for greatness—and it showed even at an early age. He learned from Potiphar; he observed Potiphar; he humbly and faithfully served Potiphar. And, more important, Joseph didn't forget about God, even if he may have felt like God had forgotten about him and allowed him to be a slave rather than the great leader he dreamed about. A true leader shows integrity, especially when it is dark and life doesn't add up to our expectations.

Even in Egypt, while Joseph was away from his beloved father and jealous brothers, God was with him and caused him to have success, even as he was in service to Potiphar (Genesis 39:2). And with his success came promotion. Joseph didn't have to lobby for a better role in Potiphar's regime—his work and the favor of God stimulated his promotion. To be promoted, the successful leader Joseph didn't have to jockey for position and share his dream of others serving him. When we are promoted simply because we have done what we should be doing, we don't have to take credit for it and we can more clearly see how God is working on our behalf. When we are promoted, we recognize God's favor in setting up the promotion as well as in giving us the gifts and skills to operate in excellence. And, if it is God who places us in the right place at the right time, how can we boast?

As servant leaders, we recognize that the favor of God follows us—and not just so we are blessed, but so others are blessed too. Because of Joseph, Potiphar's household and property were blessed and favored by God (Genesis 39:5). Joseph's very presence in Potiphar's home caused those around him to be blessed and to prosper. True leaders light up the dark wherever they go and in whatever position they are in, and others are blessed and changed and impacted by their presence. You can be a secretary, and your presence makes the office more pleasant and successful. You can be the janitor, and the prayers you murmur in each room you clean can be heard by God and prompt blessings to fall down on the occupants. A leader's very presence changes the atmosphere of a home, church, office space, playground, or classroom. It's not the title or position that characterizes a successful leader.

And so even in Egypt as the assistant to Potiphar, Joseph stepped into his leadership role, even though it didn't resemble his dream. Joseph grew and began to understand that God was in control and God was with him in the midst of slavery and in his job as an administrator for Potiphar. Leaders stick close to God, acknowledging that every good and perfect gift is from God's hand (James 1:17). And that changes us. It makes us see our work differently, it makes us see our gifts and talents in new light, and it squelches egos when they are tempted to crop up, because, again, how can we boast about the gifts God has given us and the favor God has arranged?

A Test

And like every good leader and even not-so-good ones, Joseph encountered tests of his integrity, tests of his relationship with God, tests of his ego, and tests of his leadership abilities. Because tests lurk around us each day, it is vitally important to remain

in touch with God through prayer, studying, prais-
ing, and worshiping. When Joseph encountered Potiphar's wife, he was so close to God that he couldn't
fall for her tempting offer (Genesis 39:6–20). Potiphar's wife took note of the man Joseph had become,
both outwardly and inwardly. People are naturally
attracted to leaders—especially those who are confident and have the favor of God in their lives. But
successful leaders get this; they understand that
people want a piece of them and want to be around
the favor to just get a bit of what is emanating from
inside of the leader. They also understand that everyone's intentions are not godly, so they tread lightly in
some areas. Just as Joseph did when Potiphar's wife
said: "Come to bed with me." *You are a fine young
man; we can have some fun together. You know my
husband's schedule—we can work around him.*

And the leader emerged. Joseph had grown since
the days of that dream. He didn't think about what
he could get from Potiphar's wife; he didn't even
seem to entertain the offer. He said no, not going
to happen, absolutely not. *Don't you know how good
your husband has been to me? This man entrusts me
with everything—this entire house. Why would I break
his trust? And don't you realize my story? My God has*

been right by my side all of my life. Even though I was a slave, I am now in charge of this house. Can't you see the hand of God on my life? How in the world could I break God's trust like that—to sleep with you? You might be fine, but come on, girl, you're not that fine! I've got to stay focused on my God and all God has done for me and all God has yet to do in me.

Joseph's integrity just made him look finer to Potiphar's wife. She was not used to being told no, especially by the help. So, one day, she decided to grab Joseph and go for it, but Joseph's integrity still rose: he ran away from this lustful woman—unfortunately for him, leaving his coat behind.

Smart leaders can sniff out danger. Smart leaders know when they are up against something that they can't even risk being in the same room with. Smart leaders know when they need to bring along a friend to minister or request another office or fast and pray before a meeting with a particularly attractive person. We are humans, but we know we can't fight the human urges in the physical realm. Smart leaders know their limitations with people, food, other substances. They know who they need to stay away from, and they don't play around. Joseph, recognizing how much God had done for him and even how much his mentor Potiphar had done for him, didn't play with fire. He escaped by any means necessary.

A wise pastor friend of mine, who is married, once told me that he understood the type of woman he was attracted to. He knew the style and type of women who made him raise his eyebrows, and he had identified the women in his church he could be attracted to. He didn't pounce upon these women or take advantage of his position as pastor. No, instead, he shared his issue with his closest friends and staff. He shared with them his "type" and how he needed extra help when encountering certain women; his staff knew to rush to his side whenever they saw a certain type of woman approach him. At first, my friend's protection plan seemed a bit obsessive or even weak on my friend's part. But in hindsight, I think it was smart. He knew his weaknesses, and he was wise enough to admit them. Even wiser, he had a practical plan of action to deal with his issues. He didn't place any unrealistic expectations on the women, nor did he blame them for being attractive or suggest they only wear certain clothing. He took responsibility for his own thoughts and made sure his actions were in line with his convictions, even calling for help before he needed it. What a Joseph-like leader!

Leader, do you know your trigger points? Do you know what could cause you to fall into temptation? It doesn't have to be only about sex. It could be greed, the temptation to want more and more and more. *More* is an infinite concept—you will always want more until you are content with what you have (see Philippians 4:11–13). Your temptation may be power or ego or status or appearance; know your trigger points, know your temptations, and wisely activate escape plans as quickly as possible. Find your exit now.

Success Does Not Mean Easy

And even when we escape, trouble can catch up with us. Even when we do what is right by our God and by our human leaders, trouble has a way of knocking at our door. Potiphar's wife was not happy that the fine Joseph had turned her down, and she lied about him. She used the coat he left behind in his haste to flee to show her husband that Joseph had tried to sleep with her. She stooped to another low and even called Joseph by his ethnicity and position rather than the fine and favored young man she tried to sleep with: "The Hebrew slave you brought into our house tried to come in and fool around with me" (Genesis 39:17). (Why do we turn to racial slurs in the heat of the moment? He was a Hebrew slave when she was checking him out and wanted him. He was a Hebrew slave when she propositioned him. Yet it was only when she was rejected that she named him as a Hebrew slave. Bigotry is based out of rejection and a sense of entitlement.)

So Joseph was thrown into jail. His life wasn't turning out nearly as dreamy as he expected. Yet Joseph's leadership wasn't diminished by his location. Even in prison, Joseph was a leader. He was sought out and connected to God, who gave him the gift and skill to interpret dreams. This time he used his dreams to help other servant leaders (the chief cup-bearer and the chief backer in Genesis 40) get out of jail. He accurately interpreted the dream their boss had, and with this information these servant leaders were restored to their positions. Joseph asked that they remember him when they are freed, but they don't (Genesis 40:23). Successful leaders always do remember those who helped them, especially when they were down. How dare you enjoy the fruits of living in luxury while those who helped you live in squalor and wait for liberation? How dare you enjoy the freedom and not go back to help others?

Well, as God would have it, the cupbearer was eventually forced to remember Joseph, the dream interpreter who saved them while in jail. When his boss had a tough dream and forced others to help interpret it, no one could. That's when the cupbearer thought back two years later to how he was released from prison. He told his boss about Joseph. And Joseph rose to the occasion.

This time, Joseph didn't take center stage and try to show off his gifts and skills. Joseph didn't even take credit, as if the sun and stars and moon bowed to him. Joseph said, God can give you the answer (Genesis 41:16).

The moment was right; the interpretation was correct. The leader had grown closer to God. He was in step with God. And now he was in the proper position and proper place to lead effectively and according to God's plan. Joseph told the pharaoh that his dreams all meant the same thing: God was about to give Egypt seven years of abundance followed by seven years of famine (Genesis 41:28–32). Joseph went on to advise the pharaoh, as good leaders often do. He gave the pharaoh a smart plan to make it through the next fourteen years; while there is abundance, save (a message for us all). Don't use up all you have when things are going great. Save some. Then, when the famine comes—or hard times or accidents or the unexpected—you can use what you've stored up and saved.

It was a smart plan. It was sound. It came from the lips of a mature leader. Joseph's leadership was clearly exemplified in his message and character. The pharaoh recognized the spirit of God (Genesis 41:38) in Joseph because even the ungodly can sense God's presence in a true leader's life. Pharaoh appointed this leader to implement the brilliant fourteen-year plan and to be in charge of Egypt. The little dreamer who was sold into slavery now was second only to the pharaoh in the entire land of Egypt! Only God can do that—studying hard, jockeying for position, and networking can only do so much for a leader. Successful leaders know this and rely on God for the true increase. Yes, we prepare. Yes, we see our trials as tests and stepping-stones, but in the end, we fully understand that our success is because of God. And that underlying theme will always guide us and lead us—in the boardroom, in the classroom, at home, and everywhere we go.

A Dream Realized

To bring Joseph's story full circle, I want to remind you that he did get to see his vision of his brothers bowing down to him come to pass. During those seven years of famine, Joseph's brothers were impacted too. The land they lived in, Canaan, was also hit by the famine. They had no grain, but they had heard about Egypt and how they had some left. These men, who had gotten rid of Joseph many years before, now came stumbling down to Egypt looking for food. They could never have imagined that they would be standing before their younger brother asking to be saved.

But his leadership shone through even more in his big reveal to his brothers. I can hear Joseph's words loud and clear as I read Genesis 45:1–7.

Oh my! Our Lord is real. Our God is faithful and just and amazing. Listen, guys. I am your brother. I am Joseph. Yes, I'm the one you threw in the well and then sold to the Egyptians. It's me, Joseph. Oh, don't be afraid. I'm not going to hurt you. I don't hold any grudges. Look at what God has done. I came to Egypt ahead of you for such a time as this! God knew about this famine well before we did, and God has made a way to save you and our family through me. God has gotten the glory out of this whole ordeal—we are saved because of the way things turned out. Isn't God amazing? Just when you thought you had done the worst thing in life, God turned it around and made it work out well for you and me and many others. Celebrate with me, brothers. Bring Daddy to me. We can all celebrate. Our God is worthy of all the praise we can give.

Could you be as wise and mature and forgiving as Joseph? Can you look your past square in the eye and know that God has used it—even the ugly and horrible stuff—to make you a better person, a better leader? And your journey hasn't been just for your glorification or promotion; it's always been about helping and serving others, just like Joseph did. He finally saw that being the center, being the one his brothers bowed down to, was not about his ego being enlarged; it was ultimately about service.

Leadership has an amazing way of reminding us to serve, just as Jesus did for us. He is our ultimate example of a successful leader. If you would have known you had to go through so much to be in the position you're in now, I doubt you would have wanted to brag about it. Our dreams can come true, but we never know the road we will need to take to meet up with our destiny. But when we stick close to God, we know it will turn out well for us and for those we serve.

It's the beauty of God—the beauty of being called to serve. If we're willing to persevere, we can develop into strong, wise, and God-fearing leaders.

—

Merciful and loving God: I give you praise and honor for the journey you have taken me on and continue to guide me through. I thank you for my dreams and visions, and I trust you to bring them to pass in your time and in your way. I want to be a wise and discerning leader who always gives you the credit for my abilities. Keep me humble as I look for opportunities to serve your people well. I am a wise leader, ever seeking to grow closer to your vision for my life as I grow closer to you. Amen.

Let each experience shape you and
your character.

Moses

Successful leaders make others better.

Moses answered the people, "Do not be afraid.
Stand firm and you will see the deliverance the
LORD will bring you today. The Egyptians you see
today you will never see again. The LORD will fight
for you; you need only to be still."

(Exodus 14:13–14, NIV)

But Moses sought the favor of the LORD his God.
"LORD," he said, "why should your anger burn against
your people, whom you brought out of Egypt with
great power and a mighty hand? Why should the
Egyptians say, 'It was with evil intent that he brought
them out, to kill them in the mountains and to wipe
them off the face of the earth'? Turn from your fierce
anger; relent and do not bring disaster on your people."

(Exodus 32:11–12, NIV)

As humans, we can be so great yet so flawed at the same time. Sometimes we need to be saved from ourselves, from our own self-destructive behavior and our own self-defeating actions. We can be lazy and hardworking in the same day; we can be motivated and lackluster in the same hour; we can be caring, compassionate, and loving and at the same time mean, bitter, and brutal. It takes a strong and successful leader to liberate people from themselves and their issues. When we consider the men and women of the Bible who served as examples of successful leadership, Moses is one who handled people with lots of issues; he led the complaining and discontent Israelites out of slavery in Egypt and even intervened with God for this unappreciative group. He had a tough job, and he rose to the occasion. He's arguably the greatest leader of the Old Testament, as his story has been retold over and over throughout generations. His impact on Judeo-Christian faiths is undeniable. This leader of the children of Israel from Egypt to the Promised Land of Canaan could write a handbook alone for leaders. He's known for sharing the law with the developing nation of God's chosen people—the Ten Commandments. He's known for parting the Red Sea so God's people could escape the wrath of the pharaoh. He's known for so much, but there are some specific leadership qualities I've grown to appreciate in Moses as he led the Israelites.

Moses' entire career could be summed up with the title *liberator*. From the beginning, he was on a trek to set the Israelites free from oppression. They were living in Egypt, after traveling there to live under Joseph's rule during the famine. These people had grown in number and were feared by the Egyptians. They were made slaves and forced to do hard and unmerciful labor, yet they still increased. The pharaoh was afraid of the power these people could have—so he tried several methods to suppress them. But nothing worked. He even went as far as to order every male baby killed at birth—yet they still lived. Finally, the pharaoh drew the line and said, fine, if I can't kill them in the womb or right when they are born, I want every boy killed. This will stop these people from growing (Exodus 1:8–22).

Yet even with this attempt, Moses lived. His mother put him in a basket and sent him down the Nile River. He was found by the pharaoh's daughter, who took him in and raised him as her own. So Moses was born an Israelite and raised as Egyptian royalty (Exodus 2:1–10). But he never forgot who he was. A successful leader never does; she still recalls the people she grew up with, their conditions and their needs. Likewise, Moses didn't turn a blind eye to those who were not privileged as he was. When Moses saw an Egyptian beating an Israelite slave, he reacted. He killed the Egyptian (Exodus 2:11–12). He was a voice for the powerless. Now, I'm not advocating killing a man who is oppressing another, but standing up for the oppressed exemplifies leadership. Even when you are raised with the proverbial silver spoon in your mouth, you can stand up for others. You can use your privilege and power to assist—not kill or further oppress another.

The murder Moses committed does catch up with him, as all sins tend to. Ever the liberator, Moses tried to intervene when he saw two Israelites fighting (Exodus 2:13). When he asked why a brother was hitting another brother, one of the men turned on Moses and asked, *Are you going to kill me like you killed that Egyptian?* (Exodus 2:13–14)

My mother used to always say, "What's done in the dark will come to light." She was right, of course. Even though Moses didn't think anyone had seen him stand up for the Israelite and kill the brutal Egyptian, someone had...and people talk. Word had apparently gotten around that the Hebrew man living in the Egyptian palace had struck someone dead. His intentions didn't travel with the gossip; they rarely do. Therefore, successful leaders try their best to align their actions with their intentions at all times.

Realizing that the murder he committed was not a secret, Moses fled. But, like Joseph, he ran right into God's plan for his life. It was during his escape that Moses settled in Midian. He married. He and his wife, Zipporah, had children (Exodus 2:22). He explored the land and picked up some leadership skills from his father-in-law, Jethro, a priest. It was in this land—very unlike the beauty and progressiveness of Egypt—that Moses, unbeknownst to him, was trained even more for his ultimate task of leadership. He lived in a wilderness area, the same area he would eventually lead the Israelites through. Every place we go is a place of preparation, whether we realize it or not. God knows our paths and his plans for us; perhaps the dry season in your life is the setup for the biggest and most important leadership role in your life. Sometimes it can take years upon years (forty for Moses) to get the experience and knowledge and insight we need to truly lead.

If only we could see our desert moments as preparation moments, we'd be better students. It was only after my own personal bouts with depression that I became much more caring and concerned about people who just didn't seem to live up to their potential. By staggering through my own pain and my own season in a wilderness, I became much more sensitive and aware of human needs and how certain circumstances and medical conditions can make people less productive—not because they are just lazy, but because sometimes it has taken all of their strength and will to just get out of bed. I became a better leader because of my wilderness. So it is with Moses.

Leadership Preparation

And it was in the wilderness of Midian, a dry and desolate place near the Red Sea, that Moses heard his "call" from God to put his liberation passions into practice and to good use. God had heard the cries of the Israelites, who were continuously oppressed in Egypt. And God had an answer: Moses. God told Moses that he would be the one to stand up to the new pharaoh and proclaim "Let my people go" (Exodus 3:10).

Moses resists this daunting task—who wouldn't? Some of the best reasoning on resisting my calling came when I was in seminary. Many students in seminary or those deciding whether or not to attend often wrestle with the idea of ministry. I, too, wrestled with formal training. Yet one professor said, I'd be scared if you didn't wrestle. This is serious stuff. You are tending to someone's soul. I think this advice applies to whatever you're doing for God, whether in formal ministry or not.

Leadership is like that too. You are tending to an aspect of someone's life. Moms tend to their kids' souls—huge stuff. You mess up, and you can mess up a child for life. Business deals are messing with people's livelihoods. A bad decision can trickle down quickly, disrupting a family's next meal. A student leader on campus can set the tone for the next few years, causing others to move forward or remain stagnant. It takes a lot of guts to be a good leader, and it shouldn't be a job you sign up for without weighing all of the costs. Moses did just that.

Yet God being God and certain of Moses as his

choice saw all of his potential, not his lack of skill. God was the one behind Moses. Moses may have been a murderer on the run, but he was God's instrument to liberate Israel.

And isn't that all we are as leaders: God's instruments? God can use us to do great things—but don't get it twisted; God can use anyone to do even greater things. Degrees are great. Training is essential. Mentors help. But in the end, it's God who truly provides what we need to lead.

It takes two chapters of back-and-forth with God, pleading for God to send someone else, for Moses to make his way toward Egypt to do what he was born to do: liberate the people. Moses is finally working in his passion area. After forty years of living in Midian, Moses reluctantly follows God's lead and returns to Egypt to free his people. Any good leadership advice encourages people to work in an area they are passionate about. But how do you know what your passion is? How is what you're passionate about a job, or a calling or a vocation? When we are attentive to the signs God uses—like the burning bush with Moses—we can discover the things that make us upset or the things that get us excited or the causes that make us stay up late into the night. God can and does reveal our passions if we take the time to listen and stay in tune with his promptings, even when we feel unqualified to do what God calls us to do. Somehow, God can weave together our passions with service to help us find exactly what we are placed on Earth to do. And so it was with Moses. He was called to liberate a people, to lead and guide them toward the land and life God had promised just for them. He mustered up courage to do the tough work of standing before the pharaoh and declaring that God's people must be free.

The passionate leader Moses reminded the people that God had heard their cry and would indeed set them free. Even though it didn't come easy—even after sending plague after plague, the pharaoh refused to release the slaves—Moses persevered and passionately led the people, reminding them that God had indeed heard their cries for liberation. He masterfully steps into his role and follows God's instructions, even as he leads a sometimes doubting people across the massive Red Sea.

Liberation work was Moses' sweet spot, whether he recognized it or not. Through the tribulations and the grumbling and negativity of the Israelites, Moses stood tall as a true leader. He grew to love the people he served. He protected them. He stood up for them. He went to bat for them. Do you?

A Leader People Can Trust

People want to follow someone they can trust, someone they know has their best interests at heart. How do those you serve know you care? How do they know you are passionate about making sure they are okay and have all of the tools needed to become all God has called them to be? Do you see their needs as a priority, or are you only concerned about how they can help you meet your own personal goals?

When you genuinely care about the well-being of those you serve, you take the time to know them. You take the time to learn their likes and dislikes, their own passions and goals. Because you're invested in them as people rather than as a commodity to produce more and more, you treat them as God's unique and special creation. You work to liberate them from whatever may oppress them. Leadership is service to people.

Moses grew bolder and bolder as he stepped into his calling. Putting up with the mumbles and grumbles of the very people he worked hard to serve, he often intervened on their behalf with God, the One who had called him to this task (Exodus 32: 9–14).

And as most passionate leaders do, Moses continued to give his all—so much so that his father-in-law had to step in and offer some sage advice. When Jethro visited his daughter Zipporah and her leader husband, Moses, he noticed how hard the passionate man was working. He loved the people so much that he stayed up late and woke up early to serve them. He poured himself into the people, making rulings on their cases, dispensing God's words and laws. But what Jethro saw was a leader facing burnout, and he stepped in and told Moses he had to change some things. He needed to set up a system that would help him serve the people even better, and sometimes serving means asking for help and empowering others to help you. Moses needed to focus on the big-picture issues, not the day-to-day operations of ruling Israel. Jethro told Moses to handle only the big cases because his load needed to be lighter (Exodus 18:23–24). By stepping back, Moses could actually help his people more.

Have you evaluated your effectiveness and

potential for burnout, leader? Are you the only one who can do the work at hand—or are there people around you that you can train and entrust to help you in a meaningful way? Be forewarned: empowering others means you will have to relinquish some control, and you will have to be okay with others doing things the way they see fit, not only as you see fit. If you focus on the real issue—help to serve more and more effectively—you can use your passion and energy on other, perhaps more important, needs. You can serve better when you use your help effectively.

Moses had the wisdom to listen to his father-in-law. While Jethro hadn't led a nation like Israel, he still was able to provide invaluable insight. Who do you listen to? Who is your mentor? He or she doesn't have to do the exact same job you are doing, but sometimes another person can see things you can't see because you're so passionate and close to the situation. Utilize your village for wise advice—and listen.

Leaders want to do it all and see success, but we can't want to meet goals so much that we are willing to sacrifice our own well-being. Don't you work better after a truly relaxing vacation? Don't you give more after you've had a few hours or days to unwind and process what is happening? If you're always doing and going and checking off items on the to-do list, when do you have time to reinvigorate or recharge? Even God ordained the Sabbath day as a day of rest, a day to reflect and connect. When was your last vacation, leader? When was the last time you got away from your task or your family to just sit and rest and regroup? Self-care helps you care for others better.

And you are better off if you can incorporate that self-care into every day. Whether it is morning devotions, exercise, or engaging in a beloved hobby, you lead more effectively when you actively break away.

Pastor Bill Hybels said at a Willow Creek Leadership Conference that he often ran more miles when he was busier. He knew stressful times and situations required that he pay more attention to his physical, mental, and spiritual health, so he protected his exercise routine even more when he was facing greater challenges. He was more aware of his ability to slip into an unhealthy pattern when things heated up, and he had learned coping mechanisms and effective ways to protect himself from the dangerous results of burnout.

Missteps

And just as with all success stories, Moses, our successful example, had his missteps—some with irreparable consequences. Toward the end of his reign as the great liberator, Moses was fed up with the very people he'd helped in so many ways. His anger boiled over and pushed him to strike a rock—instead of following God fully and just speaking to the rock to get the desired water for the people. Because he didn't trust God enough to do exactly what he said—as simple as it was—God told Moses that neither he nor Aaron, his brother and sidekick, would enter the Promised Land (Numbers 20:9–12). I know how Moses felt. He was tired and fed up with these people and their complaining!

Oh, you children of Israel. When will you learn? Haven't you seen all of the ways God has protected you and provided for you? Must I rehearse what God has done? You were there; you experienced it. You are the ones who cried to the Lord when you were in Egypt. You worried about crossing the Red Sea—and God opened it up. Then you thought the Egyptians would catch you—and God closed the sea on them. You worried about food— and God gave you manna. And now you are worried about water! Huh? Do you think God has brought you this far to let you die from thirst? Really? Do you think God is unable to meet your every need all of the time? Who are you people? I just don't get it. You worry about this and that—and God has already taken care of you. You don't want to move to a new level because you are scared, but how did you get to this level? You don't pursue your dreams because you are afraid…yet God gave you the dreams. I just don't get you. I've worked to take care of you, to keep you from danger, to show you God's way. And you still worry about a drop of water. Well, God has told me to command water to come out of this rock just for you, you discontented, short-sighted rebels! Take this water from the rock. I'm so tired of you all and your doubts. Let me hit this rock so the water will come out and you can be reminded yet again of who God is.

Shaking his head in disbelief, Moses let his anger get the best of him. He struck the rock—instead of simply commanding it—and water gushed out for the hard-headed people. But he'd gone too far. God didn't say to hit the rock; he just said to speak to it. God was able to get water from the rock any way God desired: Moses knew this, but emotions ran high and a bad call was made—as is expected when we act out of anger. (Ever regret those words you typed in an e-mail when angry? Breathe, stop, walk away... but do not react in anger.)

Like they were for Moses, the consequences can be too high. All of the work he'd done, all of those he had set free—and he would not get to live in the Promised Land. It's a startling reminder that we need to walk carefully next to God throughout our service. Regardless of our tenure or age, we can never take for granted our relationship with God and God's instructions. A wise and successful leader does just what God says—regardless of the ever present temptation to add more or do more for emphasis. People are tough to lead. People have lots and lots of issues. A successful leader is well aware of the human relationship issues we have to deal with—and we strive to make people better. Yet we know we can't do this alone. We need to trust God—fully. Do what God says—only.

～

God, my Help and my Leader, thank you for the people you have given me to lead in my home, at work, and in my community. I know we are all humans with human tendencies. Help me to see your love and your light in each person I serve this day. Help me to pull out the very best in your people, even when they complain and grumble. Give me the spirit of Moses to liberate people from their oppressors, even when that oppressor lives within. Give me the strength to follow you fully and trust only in your strength and power. I love you and I am honored to serve you by serving your people. Amen.

Make someone better today.

Huldah

Successful leaders say what needs to be said, regardless of the message.

So Hilkiah the priest, Ahikam, Acbor, Shaphan, and Asaiah went to the New Quarter of Jerusalem to consult with the prophet Huldah. She was the wife of Shallum son of Tikvah, son of Harhas, the keeper of the Temple wardrobe. She said to them, "The LORD, the God of Israel, has spoken! Go back and tell the man who sent you, 'This is what the LORD says…'"

(2 Kings 22:14–16, NLT)

It can be tough to say what needs to be said when you are a leader (or even just a human being trying to communicate with someone else). We live in a world that honors affirmation more than truth.

Affirmation is important, but affirmation should not come at the cost of truth. Leaders must support and affirm while still sharing what needs to be said, particularly when you can help someone grow and learn and develop. After all, isn't that what leadership is really about?

Speaking truth firmly and clearly has not always been my trademark. I've grown—a lot. I can remember when I was an editor in my twenties. I was in charge of managing freelance writers—most of whom were older than me. I wanted to affirm a particular writer so much so that I sent her a glowing report on her work even though I needed her to rewrite the assignment. This writer was a friend of my boss, and I probably was overcompensating, knowing their relationship. When I sent it back to her, it was all marked up. She got really upset with me and said I had told her the work was good. She thought I had misled her. My affirming words did not convey the truth.

In hindsight, I now know my affirming words were misleading. People want to hear affirming words; people want to be told they are great and wonderful and the best thing since sliced bread. People want to know you approve of their work and think they are doing an awesome job. It makes them feel more secure and better about themselves. But what happens when that is just not the truth? Aren't we doing more of a disservice to those we serve as leaders when we don't speak truthfully? What happens if we don't correct the new hire, and she goes off to another place and does the exact same thing? Is that helpful to her? Or what about the student who thinks he can write until he gets to a college class, his paper is ripped apart, and he is actually sent to a remedial class. It happened to one of my dear friends in college. He returned to his hometown and talked with his high school English teacher, who had given him A's on all of his papers regardless of the grammatical errors that he never learned to correct. She told him his content was so great that she overlooked the mistakes. While her comments apparently boosted my friend's ego and made him a confident writer, what good was that if he couldn't even begin taking college level writing courses as a freshman?

Communicating the Tough Stuff

Successful leaders have to learn to say what needs to be said, even when it is tough.

That's why I love the small passage of scripture in 2 Kings 22:14–20 that references the prophet Huldah. She doesn't take up a lot of space in the annals of biblical history, but she spoke volumes about successful leadership.

Huldah was a prophetess—a woman who delivers God's messages. (She was also a wife, proving even in antiquity that women can lead inside and outside of our homes.) As a prophet, Huldah was charged with delivering God's message. She was called upon to tell a group what God had said after King Josiah discovered the book of the Law that had been abandoned by the people. When the king and his charges realized that this book had been discovered, he decided to read it (a novel idea!). When King Josiah, who had become king at age eight, hears the words from scripture, he wants to change. (He, too, serves as a successful model of leadership.) Upon hearing God's Word, Josiah's heart was changed. He was repentant as he tore his clothes, realizing he and the people had strayed from their covenant with God. Isn't it great when a leader can admit wrong too?

Filled with conviction, Josiah sent the priest and a few other trusted men to inquire of the Lord to see what they must do (2 Kings 22:13). When you find out you've been doing wrong—or when you get convicted—take action promptly. It can only hurt more to continue to wallow in wrong. Real leaders grow from their mistakes.

For help, Josiah's men landed at the doorstep of Huldah, the wise leader who told it exactly like it was. She told the men exactly what she heard from God. She cut straight to the chase and delivered just what "the Lord, God of Israel" said: disaster is coming.

Huldah could have chosen to dress up her words; she could have decided to say something more pleasing to the king's ears; she could have tried to win favor with the king. But this leader had more integrity than that. She first recognized that she worked for God, not the king. No matter what the king wanted to hear, Huldah ultimately reported to God—and she desired to please God by doing exactly what God had told her to do and say.

So she talked straight. She gave the message she knew was from God. Huldah said in pretty plain language (even for biblical language): "This is what the Lord says: I am going to bring disaster on this place and its people, according to everything written in the book the King of Judah has read" (2 Kings 22:16).

This was not good news. Disaster would come to the people as a result of their disobedience. And even when there was a bit of good news for the king, it still had repercussions—and Huldah didn't mince words here either.

She gave this message to the king (Josiah): "Because your heart was responsive and you humbled yourself before the Lord when you heard what I have spoken against this place and its people, that they would become accursed and laid waste, and because you tore your robes and wept in my presence, I have heard you, declares the Lord. Therefore I will gather you to your fathers, and you will be buried in peace. Your eyes will not see all the disaster I am going to bring on this place" (2 Kings 22:19–20).

Either way it went, Huldah delivered some bad news. The people would get disaster; the king would die (although in peace).

How did this woman speak so boldly and so truthfully? Leaders of today need to know.

I hear Huldah sharing a few leadership insights for us today.

I learned early on as a prophet that my calling was not about me. I was not called to make people feel good about themselves; they were going to have to get that somewhere else. I was called to say what God said, nothing more and nothing less. I realized from observing others and their mistakes that I could get in big trouble if I veered from my mission in life. I could fall into a trap if I tried to gain favor with the kings or cut deals with others. That had danger written all over it. Yes, it could be tempting to bend the truth or add a few nice words to make someone feel better, but ultimately I wouldn't be living out my truth, and that was to say exactly what God had to say. You see, I wasn't bringing judgment on the people; I was simply saying what God had told me to say. When people did right, I told them God's words too. That's how Josiah was even able to realize he needed to live the rest of his life following God's covenant. What would have happened if I had told him everything was going to be just fine for the people of Judah? What if I had cleaned up God's words and tried to convince the people that something different would happen? How would that have helped anyone? Oh no, I worked for God. I took my cues and orders from God—and God alone. It's how I stayed true to my calling as a leader.

From the Mouth of a Woman

I am glad the Bible includes Huldah, a woman prophet, because sometimes women today who speak forthrightly are not seen as good leaders but rather aggressive and insensitive, while men can say what they mean and walk away and get results. Women leaders are sometimes held to a different set of rules and forced to tiptoe around on eggshells to say what needs to be said.

All words should come from a place of love and help and truth if we are truly Christian leaders. But we do those we are called to lead a disservice when we don't give it to them straight and make the vision plain.

Sometimes a person needs to hear the words uncut to get the point. Hurt feelings can be a by-product of straight talk, no doubt, but if the recipient of the feedback sits back and takes it in, change can come. We are in service to God to build people up and help God's people reach their full potential, and people are happier and more in tune with their true selves when they are doing their best.

You know how good it feels to be on the right path, planning, envisioning, dreaming, setting goals. When you're in your zone, you are happier, more productive, and better able to serve. Why not give those you are charged with leading that same opportunity? Recognize that your feedback can be an opportunity to propel each person to be a better person, a better version of themselves. See your feedback as a way to demonstrate truth in love. God is not pleased with everything we do and say, and if we take the time to provide godly feedback, we will help others grow and become closer to our God. What a sacred task we get to have as we work with others.

Say it. Mean it. Watch others grow.

Amazing and almighty God, give me the courage to say what needs to be said. Give me the wisdom to communicate clearly and effectively so that your people may grow and develop. Empower me to empower those you have put in my charge so that we may each grow to be the best you would have us be. Forgive me for the times I have not spoken boldly and truthfully. I desire to be a successful leader like Huldah and say what needs to be said. Amen.

Have that tough conversation—today.

King Saul and the Prophet Samuel

Successful leaders always do what God says.

Then Samuel said,
Do you think all GOD wants are sacrifices—
*   empty rituals just for show?*
He wants you to listen to him!
Plain listening is the thing,
*   not staging a lavish religious production.*
Not doing what GOD tells you
*   is far worse than fooling around in the occult.*
Getting self-important around GOD
*   is far worse than making deals with your dead*
*   ancestors.*
Because you said No to GOD's command,
*   he says No to your kingship*

(1 Samuel 15:22–23, MSG)

Successful Succession

Leaders need advisors. Let's journey back through the reigns of a noted king of Israel and a prophetic priest and advisor to glean leadership skills from their successes and mishaps.

Saul was the first king of Israel. He was the answer to the people's prayers, and he was chosen by God. (Yes, despite how his reign ends, Saul was called and handpicked by God to lead the people of Israel even though God was their divine leader (1 Samuel 8:7). Before this time, judges and prophets, like Samuel, were leading the people. But Samuel let his sons run things, and his sons were not as wise and obedient to God as he was (1 Samuel 8:3).

I've witnessed confusion and distrust in the workplace and in the church when the leader passes the baton to his son or daughter. Some children do not have the same values, morals, passions, skills, or gifts as their parents do, and parents sometimes do not see who their kids truly are. Parents can sacrifice the mission of the organization to allow their children to lead.

Samuel should have known better; he himself had

witnessed Eli, the priest who trained him, and his sons. Eli was a man of God, a servant, a leader, a priest who performed his duties honorably; however, the Bible says Eli's sons were "wicked men" (1 Samuel 2:12). They "treated the Lord's offering with contempt." These men had no respect for God, God's house, God's people, or the sacrifices brought to God. They didn't follow in their priestly father's footsteps. After observing firsthand how different Eli's sons were from their godly father, why in the world would Samuel not check his own sons?

Successful leaders would take special note of this pattern played out by Eli and then again by Samuel. Parents love their kids, but a true leader can look directly at his son's character flaws or right at her daughter's leadership skills (or lack of) and say, *You're not ready for this position. I'll do everything I can to help you get the training and the experience, but if you don't make the cut, you don't make the cut. I can't leave this organization in the hands of an untrusted or unqualified leader. While I love you as my child and will do just about anything for you, I am accountable to God first and foremost. And this organization is one I built from the ground up (or inherited from hard-working hands). I worked hard to establish myself and gain the confidence of my congregation and staff, so I just can't leave this to you by way of bloodline. You're going to have to work and prove yourself if you want this business. I have to answer to God for my decisions, and I can't entrust the people I serve to just anyone—even my own flesh and blood.*

A successful leader can honestly assess his child's gifts and strengths and either groom them adequately for the position (even if that means having them work their way up through the ranks) or choose a successor better suited to the needs of the organization. A successful leader can make a tough choice. The mission of the organization surpasses the hurt feelings of the child or the parent.

Instead of learning from Eli's blind loyalty to his sons, Samuel followed in his footsteps and apparently appointed his sons to run the priestly business. And the people had to call Samuel on his mistakes. The people had to tell the priest that his sons were not fit for the job. They showed up and said directly, "You are old, and your sons do not walk in your ways; now appoint a king to lead us, such as all the other nations have" (1 Samuel 8:5). The Israelites might have wanted a king anyway—they liked doing what other nations did regardless of their special relationship with God—but they used Samuel's misstep to ask for a king. They declared that they couldn't possibly follow Samuel's sons, who took bribes and refused to administer justice (1 Samuel 8:3). Israel used their wrongs to get what they really wanted. Yet another reason for leaders to always be mindful of their relationship with God: they can't afford to have too many wrongs because others will use them to further their own agendas.

Israel used Samuel's sons as an excuse to request a king even though they had God ruling and reigning over them through God's priests and prophets. Our need to be successful can make us peer over at what our neighbors have and want it. Stay focused on all God has given you, leader.

God granted the Israelites their wish and told Samuel to let the people know what they were getting. Like all good leaders, God (and Samuel) told the people the consequences of their request. God instructed Samuel to say: *Your king will be a taskmaster. Don't think you're getting off easy by asking for an earthly king; he will be a man with human frailties. Listen up: this king you are asking for will make you work and will make you serve him. Who else do you think will escort him around town and drive his chariots? You and your children will be servants to your king. He's going to make everyone work. Whether it's in the army, or in the fields, or in the home, you all will have to work. And when you produce really good crops or really good wares, your king will not let you keep these things. The king will take the very best you produce and give it to his court for their enjoyment. He will expect at least a tenth of everything you earn, and he's not going to ask kindly—he will take it. But you don't want God to rule over you. You never have. You have turned your backs on me throughout history, even when I rescued you from that pharaoh in Egypt. But Israel, I'll give you just what you ask for, even though I know that you will not like it. You will not be treated well, and then you will cry out to me. But know that I've already warned you. You want a king, you get a king.*

Even with the harsh warning delivered by Samuel to the people, they cried out to God:

Oh no, we want a king. We want what everybody else has. Who needs Yahweh over you when you can have a man, a royal king to lead you and guide you and help you win your battles? Give us a king—now!

Be careful what you pray for. (Well, that's true!)

And enter the first king of Israel—Saul. Saul fit the physical bill quite well. He was described as "impressive...without equal among the Israelites." He stood out. He was taller than anyone else—at least by a foot. Woe to a leader who is judged by his or her looks alone!

Humility and Anonymity

Even though they had rejected God, God knew Saul could lead his people against one of their formidable enemies, the Philistines (1 Samuel 9:16).

Saul, however, didn't feel worthy of the honor. There's something endearing about his humility (1 Samuel 9:21). Saul knows he's not from a royal family; he's from the smallest class of the smallest tribe. He feels insignificant and unworthy. When we are called to lead in our homes, churches, businesses, communities, shouldn't we have a bit of humility? Our résumés may look great, but isn't there always someone else who has a better one? Our family may have been in the business, but isn't there a better person outside of the organization or perhaps even within who could also lead? Humility as Christian leaders is essential. While egos stink in the secular world, you've not smelled ego unless you've sniffed it out in the church, in a Christian organization, or among Christian leaders. It is foul! The very nature of who we are as Christians—followers of Christ, who sacrificed his life for ours—should make us stop dead in our tracks, rip up our accolades, and humbly say, *I am not worthy of this job, yet I'll go because you have called me, Lord.* When you are tempted to think you deserve a position or deserve respect or deserve to be in a certain place, compare yourself to our model, Jesus Christ. You will come up sufficiently lacking. Learn from Saul's humility, even if he didn't keep it throughout his reign. We are all unworthy, yet we are called to a sacred task of leadership by God, who can make us more than capable of doing the job.

And Saul has another key element of true leadership: he is anointed by God. In 1 Samuel 10, Samuel anointed the new king with oil and proclaimed that the Spirit of the Lord was with him. God had chosen him, God anointed him. God would lend his Holy Spirit to rest upon him and guide him and lead him (if he only listened). Leaders are called, leaders are anointed, leaders are made capable by God's Holy Spirit.

Take a self-inventory right now. Are you operating under God's spirit each and every day, through each and every decision? A successful leader knows that stepping outside of God's will can bring destruction. While we can be tempted to push an issue, do things our way, and think we know best, our best position is prayer. We pray, pray, pray over all decisions. We pray, pray, pray throughout the day, seeking God's will for every move we make. We don't get paralyzed, unable to make a decision because we're waiting on the big sign from God, but we do communicate regularly with God. If we somehow make a mistake or step outside of God's spirit, we know we're not too far from God to right our wrongs.

Staying close to God is the only way to be a successful leader. Staying under the anointing of God's powerful Holy Spirit is the only way to deal with the demons raging inside and outside of us. *Holy Spirit, come and live and rest right here with me and each step I take. Whisper in my ear and let me know where to go and how to go and when to respond and how to respond.*

It's not you, it's God.

Under God's anointing, Saul had some good and successful years as Israel's first king. He urged the people to avoid killing on a day proclaimed as the day God rescued Israel (1 Samuel 11:13). He respected God and recognized God as the giver of the victories of Israel. Saul was also wise enough to keep Samuel close. Saul recognized Samuel as a priest and prophet sent by God. True leaders know who they can trust—who is truly sent by God.

Yet soon Saul fell for several reasons.

A Formula for Failure

First, Saul let the people's fear become his fears. In 1 Samuel 13, the Israelites were facing their formidable enemy, the Philistines. When a soldier (Jonathan) was victorious in a battle against the Philistines, the enemies naturally planned to retaliate. They came with numbers (1 Samuel 13:5); they pulled out all of the stops when they saw that the Israelites were tough despite their size and number. And the Israelites got scared—probably for good reasons. This was where they needed their godly leader. But Saul caved. Saul began by asking for the prophet Samuel, and Saul even waited seven days for Samuel (1 Samuel 13:8). Saul had his mind in the right place; he thought the people needed the priest (Samuel) to offer sacrifices to the Lord to face the giant Philistines. Saul wanted to seek God, and he called for his help (Samuel), but his help didn't come within the time frame Saul thought was appropriate. He panicked. Oh, how we are like Saul! We know we should wait on God, we know we should wait until the time looks right and feels right according to our internal spirit, but sometimes we can't wait.

So Saul went ahead and made the offering himself, which was against the commandment. Samuel says when he does show up (1 Samuel 13:13), "You acted foolishly."

Oh, Saul. Why couldn't you just wait until I showed up? Have I ever not come when you called before? Just because I don't run down at the exact moment you think I should doesn't mean I'm not coming. Why did you let these people make you forget who is really in charge and able to fight the largest of enemies? Oh, Saul.

And like that, Saul's downward spiral began. His

reign would not last (1 Samuel 13:13); God would find another man, someone after his own heart (1 Samuel 13:14) to reign as king.

One misstep, one time listening to the wrong people, one time jumping the gun can lead us down a spiral that will negatively impact our leadership. People won't remember the times we followed God or the times we did exactly what we were called to do; things can spiral downhill quickly. Stick close to God, seek forgiveness quickly when needed, and stay close to God and godly people. Leaders need them.

Knowing God's spirit has left him, Saul turned wicked. Thankfully, if we repent, we don't have to endure this type of torture. Saul put unreasonable demands on the people (1 Samuel 13:24), which is the surest way to become an ineffective leader quickly. And this leader, who was once anointed and chosen by God, became one who grieved God (1 Samuel 15:11).

How could stepping ahead of God once lead to such destruction? A word to the wise: be careful when you make one misstep; another is lurking around the corner.

Samuel had to let Saul know that he had been

rejected by God. Samuel had to deliver the unpleasant news—and he did.

Saul, I'm sorry and God is so sorry that he has made you king. You've messed up. Big time. You started out well, but it is more about how you finish. God told you to do one thing: to destroy the Amalekites totally. But no, you decided to only do half of the job. You wanted their goods for yourself. You didn't think God would continue to provide everything you and Israel needed. How could you let greed take you down such a path? I know it started out with one little thing and then it blossomed into full-blown awful disobedience. Oh, Saul, I wish you would have been more careful. You could have been such a good king. But God does not look for offerings and sacrifice. God prefers obedience. It's so much better to just do what God says rather than try to make some big sacrifice. It's all God's anyway. God hates rebellion—it points to your ego and arrogance, which God also hates. How dare you think you know more than God? How dare you think you can change God's plans and do just some of it and then some of what you want? How arrogant. Because of your sin—because you have rejected God's will—God has rejected you. It's a wrap. You're not going to be king much longer.

An Act of Compassion

Then, in an exemplary leadership move, Samuel had compassion on the wayward Saul and agreed to return with him to Israel. Samuel was firm and tough when he delivered the message, but he also had compassion on Saul, who said he was repentant. Samuel couldn't change God's mind, as God is not a man (1 Samuel 15:29), but he could journey with Saul. And we, as leaders, may not be able to turn back the punishment for disobedience for ourselves or those we serve, but we can journey next to them and provide a level of comfort our presence can bring.

The walk of shame is hard. True leaders will be able to walk with other leaders who are disgraced. We will be able to offer support and advice, hopefully in a manner that brings about repentance and a desire to walk down a godly path. But successful leaders know that it is not ours to decide the path the fallen leader decides to take. We give them our best, we talk with them, we guide them, we lead by example. If they veer off track, maybe one day they will remember our leadership and see our example as a guiding light toward the way. We can only plant the seeds. Someone else may bring the rain. And ultimately it is God who will make them grow. Do your job well, leader. And leave the rest to God, being ever so careful to listen to God every step of the way.

———

O, merciful Lord, I desire to follow you fully. Keep my mind upon you so that I may follow you each step of the way. I don't want to lead without you. I don't want to serve without you. I need your sweet Holy Spirit to reign and rule over my life, my work, my ministry, and my home. Help me to stay under your anointment each and every second of this day. When I am tempted to turn away, grab me and bring me to my senses quickly. I do not want to walk this path without you. I am grateful for my calling and desire to please you always. Amen.

Pray about every decision you make.

King David and Nathan

Successful leaders desire to be right
with God—first.

Create in me a clean heart, O God; and renew a
right spirit within me.

(Psalm 51:10, KJV)

Leaders need advisors. Let's journey back through the
reigns of another noted king of Israel and a prophetic
priest and advisor to glean leadership skills from their
successes and mishaps.

David was arguably the most celebrated king of
Israel's history, the most celebrated (and quoted)
leader in the Bible besides our Lord and Savior Jesus
Christ. And in many ways his leadership foreshad-
owed the type of king Israel awaited in Christ. So,
upon initial glance, David was an outstanding and

successful leader, one to be emulated, quoted, and followed.

But David wasn't all perfect. He had some serious issues, but still he was a great leader and a great king. Surely his story—his victories and his failures—can lend insight into our journey toward successful leadership.

Let's begin with the positives, his successes. David was close to God—and even during his failures, David stayed close to God throughout his life. David developed a relationship with God as a young boy. We know this because David credits God for taking care of him when he was a little shepherd (1 Samuel 17:34–37). David didn't discount his internship as a shepherd boy. He knew that he needed God to guide him and protect him as he did the lowly yet vitally important job of watching his father's sheep. David took seriously his charge to protect the sheep from lions and bears. And he took seriously the fact that God had given him the courage and strength to protect his sheep from such dangerous beasts. So, when David saw the army of Israelites afraid of the giant Goliath, David simply recalled what he learned as a boy: *God will help me fight the battle.* David wasn't proclaiming some supernatural miracle without putting forth action. No, David was actually activating his faith by saying he could fight Goliath—not because David was so great but because God is, and David's faith and history assured him that God could fight (and win) this battle too. David proclaims, "The Lord who delivered me from the paw of the lion and the paw of the bear will deliver me from the hand of this Philistine."

David used the experiences he gained as a shepherd boy to propel him during the next trial he faced. We leaders should be so in tune with God that we hear in our minds a line from one of my favorite Tye Tribbett songs: "If he did it before, he can do it again." David, as successful leaders do, realized that it was a different day on the calendar, but he still served the same God. Goliath was a giant, not a bear or a lion, but God was still able to take down whatever stood in David's way. David took God seriously and remembered all God had done. And David was wise enough to know he didn't need any special equipment to do what God needed him to do; the biggest armor he needed was his faith and trust in God's ability.

Leader, think about all that God has brought you through, all that God has allowed you to come through—not because of your smarts or strength, but because God decided to do it. Use that information to tackle today's giant, whatever it may be. Use your faith files to pull up reminders that God is in control and that you are close to God and seeking God each step of the way.

A Clean Heart

David was also a man after God's heart (1 Samuel 13:14 alludes to this). David had a heart that was like God's—that's a huge glimpse into why this man was a successful leader! David must have been loving and compassionate and generous and steadfast— only a few of God's characteristics. David had to be creative and strong and courageous. Can you imagine being a person God even says himself is after his own heart? It's a great aspiration—to have your heart so in tune with God that it resembles God—and God says so.

Leader, your heart has to be clean and pure and always seeking to follow God's will. You may not *do* right all of the time, but your heart must be desiring the right thing. David was not perfect, but even in his imperfection, even in his sin, he desired for his heart to be right (Psalm 51:10).

Our hearts often need cleaning up. The heart is where the root, the source, of our intentions rest. Leader, know your motives, check your heart (see Matthew 15:18–19). If your heart is not right, nothing else can be right. Recognize that you often need to clean up your intentions in order to pursue what's right.

A Leader Regardless of Title

Another admirable characteristic of David as a successful leader is that he is humble and ready to serve, regardless of his title. In 1 Samuel 16:14–23, we see David ministering to Saul through his music even though David had already been anointed as the next king. Saul, who was still king at that point, needs someone to soothe his evil and wicked spirit since God's presence had left him. David humbly served the man he would succeed.

When David valiantly slayed Goliath—while the armed Israelite army was shaking in their boots— he was already anointed the next leader of Israel.

Yet he fought. He served not as king but as one who wanted to stop the bully threatening his people. Even though the Spirit of the Lord had descended on David and prompted Samuel to anoint this young man as king, he was not elevated to that position just yet. He was busy serving and waiting his turn. He was humbly serving as a music therapist to the wicked king. He was busy running errands for his father and serving food to his brothers (that's actually how he found out that Goliath was threatening the Israelites [1 Samuel 17:12–24]). How many of us in leadership boldly and cheerfully do the menial stuff? How many of us believe leadership is about others serving us? How many leaders actually think we have to be in control and call the shots? What if we viewed our service as David viewed his and do what needs to be done when it needs to be done, regardless of how trivial the task at hand. What if we lead from any position we hold while joyfully and willing giving our all, showing others our faith is in God and we are willing to do whatever it takes to get things done?

My sister is a registered nurse, and she's all about patient care. She has turned down several management opportunities because she prefers to work directly with patients. She can't understand how some nurses can walk into a room and not meet the needs of the patient, even if it means performing tasks that are not their job. My sister has been known to mop up urine, change sheets, or brush a patient's hair if that's what is needed. She knows her main job is to administer medicine and other things she's been trained for while assistants take care of the "chores," yet she can't walk into a room and not serve a patient. If you ask anyone who has had her as a nurse, she's a leader in the nursing field, caring for God's people, whether she has a title or not.

Leading in a Dysfunctional System

Another characteristic of David's leadership is that he served Saul and his dysfunctional system even though David was well aware that he had been called and anointed to be king himself. He had already been chosen and confirmed by Samuel, yet he didn't push God's hand and take the kingdom by force. David waited his turn. David waited in line and in order— even though he probably would have been justified in arranging a coup. (Saul had lost it by then and was doing all sorts of crazy maneuvers, even trying to take David's life [1 Samuel 19:1]). True faith believes, like David apparently did, that even in a dysfunctional organization or family or church, God is operating. A successful leader will move only when God says move. Dysfunction doesn't call the shots; God does.

A true leader also realizes there is something to be learned even in disorder and disarray. As Saul's assistant, David had a ringside seat to the kingdom before he took the reins. Even while soothing the king's evil spirit with music from his harp, David was able to look around and see the place where he would reign soon. He could use this time to observe the system, silently take notes about changes needed, win favor from the staff (like Saul's own son Jonathan), and so on. There's probably more to learn within a dysfunctional system than there is in one that is operating smoothly. What have you observed as a follower, as an assistant, as a mere fly on the wall? That information can be used in your service to others: what you won't do, how not to treat people, how to avoid the missteps of your predecessor. There's wisdom in learning from everyone else's mistakes—then you won't need to make them for yourself.

Oh, King Saul, I know you're crazy. I can feel the

demons raging inside of you. I don't have to take you out; you're doing a good job of it yourself. I don't have to rush to be king; I'm getting a great deal of experience observing how not *to be king. I'll play my harp for you, because I want you to feel better. I'll fight in the war for you, because I want to protect God's people. I'll do whatever you ask me to do, because I'm in service to God, and this is where I'm supposed to be for now. My time is coming. You see, I trust God and God alone. My God has kept me safe this long; why should I think God will do anything differently now? I'll watch you and wait to be king. God has already said it. I've just got to wait for my time. And I may as well help you out while I'm waiting!*

Sometimes it is just not our time to be in charge; it's our time to learn and listen and observe and share our gifts in the most humbling circumstances. Saul liked David. Saul cherished David. Saul needed David. He appointed David to be a part of his armor-bearer service—giving David an even closer view of the kingship. Soon after, David became a bit too popular and Saul became jealous. But David kept serving, regardless of the craziness surrounding him (1 Samuel 18:5–16).

David's heroic efforts go on and on throughout

1 Samuel and 2 Samuel, and some of his history is also recorded in the beginning of 1 Kings and in 1 Chronicles.

Owning Up to Missteps

Yet David's story doesn't just include his victories. David is human, with a great big repentant heart that resembles God's heart. Like many leaders, David starts off strong—very strong! He moves from shepherd boy to minstrel for King Saul to head of staff. He transitions from serving his father in the pastures to working side by side with the king of Israel. He fights hard; he conquers giants; he is a celebrated leader who trusts and follows God. Yet he is human and he slips and falls several times.

One of his notorious falls is recorded in 2 Samuel 11. It involves a woman, Bathsheba. She's bathing, and David catches a glimpse of her. He doesn't turn his head when he realizes how beautiful this woman is; he doesn't gather his battle clothes and focus on work (the job at hand since his troops are off at war). No, David continues to let his desire fester in his mind and allows his lustful side to take over.

David doesn't catch his lust. We know sin starts off as a quick look or thought that if left unchecked can grow like a weed into a full-blown plant.

David asks about the woman; he summons the woman; he sleeps with the woman. Classic pattern. The woman gets pregnant, and since her husband is at war (like the rest of the soldiers except the leader, King David), she can't even pin it on her husband. But David, missing out on yet another chance to repent, falls further and summons her husband home so he can sleep with his wife and later believe the child is his.

But Uriah, another successful leader in the Bible, is a better man at this point than David is. Uriah comes home as commanded, but he doesn't go into his house; he doesn't want to sleep with his wife and lose focus on the battle.

Since Uriah wouldn't sleep with his wife and "get her pregnant," David sends an order back with Uriah (the good man carries his own death notice) that he be put on the front line, where he will be killed. When Uriah is killed, David takes his wife, Bathsheba, as his own. Sin has crept in, and David has refused to repent, so he goes down the path hard and fast.

Bathsheba has the baby, but the child becomes ill. During the illness, David prays and cries out to the Lord. Through his trusted advisor's (Nathan) words, David has already realized his sin and has sought and received forgiveness. Yet the consequences are real. David's house will not have peace, and the child will not live.

David's return to God is guided by his mentor and prophet, Nathan. Every successful leader needs trusted mentors and prophets—the ones who say exactly what needs to be said, not what we want to hear. We need the wise ones who know how to get our attention and set us straight when needed.

Nathan doesn't walk into this story and shame David and point his finger at him. He wisely tells David a story, a parable about a rich man and a poor man. Nathan appeals to David's tendency for justice. And within that parable, David sees himself. Within that story, David realizes his sin. And he repents.

Nathan knows what David needs, and he's not afraid to present it to him so he'll get it. Nathan is courageous; he could have been killed for serving up the truth to the king. But Nathan seeks to do right over doing what is safe. Do you know how to get the attention of those who you serve? It takes studying them and getting to know them and caring so deeply about them that you want to give them information in a manner that will help them become their best. Your sharing is not to bring harm or destruction, even when it is a serious warning. Your message is always about helping them become what God has destined for them to become.

David, the one with the heart like God's, hears and receives... and repents. And that is how we get to Psalm 51:

> *Have mercy upon me, O God, according to thy lovingkindness: according unto the multitude of thy tender mercies blot out my transgressions.*
> *Wash me thoroughly from mine iniquity, and cleanse me from my sin.*
> *For I acknowledge my transgressions: and my sin is ever before me.*
> *Against thee, thee only, have I sinned, and done this evil in thy sight: that thou mightest be justified when thou speakest, and be clear when thou judgest.*
> *Behold, I was shapen in iniquity; and in sin did my mother conceive me.*
> *Behold, thou desirest truth in the inward parts: and in the hidden part thou shalt make me to know wisdom.*

*Purge me with hyssop, and I shall be clean: wash
me, and I shall be whiter than snow.*

*Make me to hear joy and gladness; that the bones
which thou hast broken may rejoice.*

*Hide thy face from my sins, and blot out all mine
iniquities.*

*Create in me a clean heart, O God; and renew a
right spirit within me.*

*Cast me not away from thy presence; and take not
thy holy spirit from me.*

*Restore unto me the joy of thy salvation; and
uphold me with thy free spirit.*

*Then will I teach transgressors thy ways; and
sinners shall be converted unto thee.*

*Deliver me from bloodguiltiness, O God, thou
God of my salvation: and my tongue shall sing
aloud of thy righteousness.*

*O Lord, open thou my lips; and my mouth shall
shew forth thy praise.*

*For thou desirest not sacrifice; else would I give it:
thou delightest not in burnt offering.*

*The sacrifices of God are a broken spirit: a broken
and a contrite heart, O God, thou wilt not despise.*

*Do good in thy good pleasure unto Zion: build
thou the walls of Jerusalem.*

Then shalt thou be pleased with the sacrifices of righteousness, with burnt offering and whole burnt offering: then shall they offer bullocks upon thine altar.

We as leaders are human. We as leaders will fall and make mistakes and get sidetracked. It is foolish to think otherwise. Yet when our hearts are right and in tune with God, we can be like David and repent quickly. We can ask for restoration and walk humbly with God. We can take ownership for our actions—and use our stories to bless even more people. How many people have been touched by Psalm 51? How many more people have recited and quoted and been comforted by David's words? His life wasn't perfect, but it was still redeemable—by God.

Oh, to be a leader like David.

—

God, my Rock and my Fortress, give me a heart like yours. Make my heart pure and right. Help me to see those I serve as your amazing creations. Help me to work in partnership with you to guide and lead others into their purpose and calling. I desire to see everyone I serve know you fully and walk fully in all you have called them to do. Show me how to lead. Show me how to guide. Show me how to humbly follow you and stay close to you so sin won't be able to take me down a dangerous path. I'm your servant, open and available to do what you tell me to do. Amen.

Evaluate your motives frequently. Ask God for a clean heart.

Tabitha

Successful leaders serve, first and
foremost.

In Joppa there was a disciple named Tabitha (in
Greek her name is Dorcas); she was always doing
good and helping the poor.

(Acts 9:36, NIV)

Leader is a broad description for a person. Leaders
can be top CEOs, and leaders can be community
organizers. A successful leader can be the Sunday
school teacher who passionately creates new ways
to communicate God's love to children or a mama
who prays with her children each night. A successful leader can be a preacher, a pastor, or simply a
neighbor or friend who impacts others' lives. But one
thing about leaders stands out: service.

Successful leadership is about how we serve, how we influence others, how we care for others, and how we help others become all they are destined to be. Leadership is about helping.

Tabitha, one woman with a short passage of scripture devoted to her story, exemplifies true leadership. She is described as a disciple, which means she followed Christ. She probably came to know about Christ through the evangelism of Philip or Peter, leaders instrumental in telling people about the saving power of Christ and setting up early churches throughout Rome and parts of Africa and Asia. Their work was not in vain. Tabitha heard and received the good news. She took seriously her call as a Christian and was named a follower, or disciple, of Christ. She modeled her life after Christ's service. How closely do you model Jesus each day? How well do you know the words Jesus spoke and follow the example he lived while on earth? How often do you confer with Jesus on everyday issues as a leader? Whether it's deciding on a school for your child, what to say to your mate and how to say it, or whether to pursue the big deal, successful leaders know that they cannot make decisions without first consulting God. They understand that their service is ultimately to

God, and they can't make a move without first consulting their real boss.

Sometimes just a talk with the One we should follow ever so closely before we open our mouth will remind us that the timing is not right. Or it may give us a different perspective on a subject we are about to broach. We may remember to choose our words carefully, choose our time carefully, because we are here to serve, and even if we have to say something difficult, we want it to be received well, so that the person may grow from it, not retort or retreat.

Known by Her Actions

Tabitha is also described as one who was "always doing good and helping the poor." It's as if her actions were her name; they describe who she was. No one mentions her degrees or the organizations she belonged to or how many awards she had received. The most important part of her résumé follows her name—and it is the fact that she was consistently helping other people, particularly the poor. How's your attitude when called to serve? Do you cheerfully participate in activities that help others or are not about you or your cause? Would people say your name in synonym with service? Help? Care?

Tabitha saw her job as that of a servant. She saw her life calling as one who was to take care of those who were unable to provide for themselves. She particularly cared for widows, women who were usually left without money or land or anyone to care for them in a patriarchal society where women didn't have any rights. Tabitha, who was also known as Dorcas, took care of people who were considered the least of these; she took care of those who were least likely to ever be able to repay her kindness. The mark of a successful leader is how he handles those who cannot repay him. How does she treat the ones who cannot give her a positive review? How do you treat those who can give you nothing in return? Do you even notice them? Do you see their eyes? Do you touch them? What do you give those who will never repay you?

Tabitha, how did you do it?

I always loved to make beautiful clothes. It was my gift. When I was little I always loved beautiful fabric. I'd help my mom spin yarn and dye cloth to make beautiful fabric for others. As I grew older, I developed my gift of piecing together fabric and creating wonderful garments. Then one day, I heard about a man who had also been able to take old things and make them new. I heard about Jesus. I learned how he changed people's hearts. I heard how he healed and helped people. I had to hear more about this Jesus. I soon found out that he was actually the Messiah, the one Israel had been awaiting so long. I was amazed by all I heard about Jesus. He died for our sins, for all who believed. When I realized this, I gladly accepted Jesus and decided to follow him. And when I followed him, I couldn't help but serve other people. It's almost as if I needed to do good because the Lord had done good by giving me Jesus. I needed to help those widows I met. They had no one to take care of them, and I knew it pleased God. I needed to share all that I made with those who didn't have. I didn't even think about it. I just gave. When someone needed clothes, I was happy to provide them. I gave them my best too. I wanted others to feel beautiful when they put on my clothes, so even though I wasn't selling my clothes, I made sure I chose the best yarn and fabric to make the widows feel special. They needed some love and comfort, and I figured, if I could cheer them up just a little bit, why shouldn't I? It was all because of my joy and peace I found in Jesus. That's what made me do good and help others. It was the least I could do to say thank you to Jesus.

Tabitha never expected to be paid for her generosity, but she was. When Tabitha became ill and died, people showed up and displayed what she had given them. They showed Peter, who they summoned to come to the dead woman's side. Peter was in a nearby town sharing the gospel, but he went to see about the generous Tabitha. When he arrived, he saw the grieving people; they were distraught because Tabitha was no longer alive. (What a remarkable example. These women were not her family members, but they grieved as if they had lost their best friend. What a testimony to the way she treated the poor!) The women showed him robes and clothes that Tabitha had made and generously given to them. She didn't set up shop in the finest locations and trade with wealthy merchants. No, she saw a need and she used her talents to fulfill that need. She used her talents to serve the needs of others.

Tabitha teaches leaders to help selflessly, to donate our time and our wisdom and our gifts without seeking a return. There is a return, but it probably won't come from the pro bono case we take on or the volunteer group we serve or the people we don't charge for our services—they usually can't pay. God sees our service (Galatians 6:7–9). When we give our best and serve from our best (not the leftovers), we are taken care of. I've seen this law of reciprocity time and time again. If you make a donation, something else comes your way. If you volunteer your time, you get supernatural energy to complete a project. If you discount a service to someone in need, another comes and offers you more than your rate. It's one way God says, *I see you. I see your service, leader. I see how you didn't take shortcuts, use different fabric, give your leftovers to the one who couldn't pay you, so I'm sending the one who can pay you with some extra. No, you can't predict it. No, you can't look around the corner and see how it's coming, but you can trust and believe it will come. In fact, don't even focus on how you're going to get repaid. Just serve, and serve well. I've got the rest taken care of.*

When Tabitha got sick and died and the people she had helped showcased what she had done for them, Peter was touched by their grief. Peter, a disciple of Christ himself, who had received commissioning to heal and raise from the dead, prayed for this servant leader. He cleared her room of mourners—those she had dutifully served and those who were disturbed by their loss. He knelt and prayed to God Almighty. Peter petitioned God on behalf of this servant, and she was resurrected. She was given life again. She was given another chance to live and to serve. She got up, much like Peter's mother-in-law in Matthew 8:14–16, and served.

When service is ingrained in you like it was in Tabitha, you have nothing to do but to serve. *Yes, I was dead a few minutes ago, but now I'm alive. I've got more work to do. I've got more robes to sew and more garments to put together. Don't you see these people who need my gifts and skills? I could sit around and figure out how to get a profit, or I could go out and meet the needs right where they are. I'm not worried about my pay; I've received it. I know I'll be taken care of; it's been proven. I need to serve and care for those who need me the most.*

Do you give your second best to God in service to others? Is the same creativity provided as when you are being paid for a job?

Tabitha gave her best to those she served without one iota of expectation. She gave from her heart. We, leaders at home, in the church, in the community, would do well to emulate Tabitha's attitude and give our best, even when we are volunteering.

Leader, hope to be on the right on the day of judgment, where the King says, take your inheritance, the kingdom prepared for you since the creation of the world. For I was hungry and you gave me something to eat, I was thirsty and you gave me something to drink, I was a stranger and you invited me in, I needed clothes and you clothed me, I was in prison and you came to visit me.

And when the people asked when had they done all of this for the Lord, he replied: "Truly I tell you, whatever you did for one of the least of these brothers and sisters of mine, you did for me" (Matthew 25:40, NIV).

Service to others is service to God. It has to be your best.

—

Thank you, God, for the ability to serve your people. Thank you for the gifts you've imparted in me and given me the wisdom and skills to develop. Help me not think these gifts are to build up myself or to only make my life better. Pour into me the spirit of Tabitha so I may be generous: free to give of my time, my skills, and my resources to help your people. I want to feed you. I want to clothe you. You are welcomed in my life. I want to do my best for you and all I serve. Amen.

Give generously of your time, talent, and money.

Phoebe

Successful leaders embody their vision.

> I commend to you our sister Phoebe, who is a
> deacon in the church in Cenchrea. Welcome her
> in the Lord as one who is worthy of honor among
> God's people. Help her in whatever she needs, for
> she has been helpful to many, and especially to me.
> (Romans 16:1–2, NLT)

I grew up in the church watching both my father
and mother take their duties as deacon and deaconess seriously. They prayed for people often; they
visited the sick often; they offered rides to people
who didn't have other transportation. My parents
were not rich and didn't have very many financial
resources to share, but they served. Mom baked cakes
and delivered food to those who were ill or bereaved.

On several occasions, I remember our home being opened to someone in need. We didn't have the luxury of a guest room—with three children and two adults, our modest three-bedroom home was full. But we did have a sofa and floor space, so when someone needed a place to stay, we made room.

My mom gathered white garments and distributed them to baptismal candidates, whom she prepared for the service where they would make an outward symbol of their commitment to die to their old selves and be raised with Christ, vowing to live as followers and believers of Jesus. Mom ironed the tablecloths used for communion service. Dad purchased grape juice and saltine crackers (items we thought were a treat when they brought the leftovers home). Even watching them work, I didn't fully understand what being a deacon and deaconess meant. I thought they were the leaders of the church, the ones who got to sit up front dressed in dark suits and white dresses, while the rest of the congregation scrambled to find a seat.

But when I grew older, my vision of a deacon grew too. My church in Chicago ordained deacons the first Sunday of every December—after a long process of learning and training and serving. The new deacons stood before the church and recited answers to various questions. I was intrigued to see as many women standing before the congregation as men (oftentimes more women than men). I was even more intrigued to find out that these women would be ordained as deacons, not deaconesses. My church didn't separate the duties a man or a woman could perform. In fact, the pastor, serving as administrator of the oral test, specifically asked the deacon candidates if women could be deacons and what scriptures they would use to support their answer. Because tradition dies hard—and this little Baptist girl from a small Southern town was used to tradition—I listened with some suspicion, sitting up straighter in my seat and leaning in to make sure I heard the answers correctly. For the first time, I heard about Phoebe in Romans. I quickly wrote down the scripture the deacons recited and vowed to read about this deacon as soon as I got home.

And sure enough, right there in Romans 16 is her story. A woman. A deacon. Someone the writer Paul entrusted and submitted to the church, despite his sometimes controversial reports on women and limitation of their duties in the church. He told the people to take care of her and to give her whatever she needed. Why? Because she was a great servant (deacon) to many people, and she had even helped him.

Paul, who seemed to write that women should be subservient (Titus 2:5), quiet in church (1 Corinthians 14:35), and second to men (Ephesians 5:22–24), was saying this woman was a deacon. (Translations variously use *deacon, servant, deaconess.*)

But what made Phoebe's leadership so special that she is recognized in scripture? She knew that successful service meant embodying the message you bear. Paul and Phoebe and many others followed this new way called Christianity. They told people about Jesus Christ, who had come in the flesh and showed us a new way to live, a new way to treat people. Christ had come and turned the system upside down. Instead of an eye for an eye, Christ said turn the other cheek (Matthew 5:38–40). Instead of stoning, Christ said forgive (John 8:11). Instead of separation, Christ said unite. Christ's message was—and still is—radical. And followers of Christ should look like that message, much like Phoebe did.

A Living Letter

I'm certain that Phoebe was like the living letter Paul writes about in 1 Corinthians 3:2–4. She not only carried the message of Christ to the people—as she was believed to be carrying a letter with instructions to the Romans—but she was an example for them to see, right in front of their eyes, much like my parents were to me. Phoebe showed up with a letter in her hand, but even if no one read the letter, they could get its message just from seeing her in action. She embodied her message.

As one of the earliest women to be entrusted with such a high honor and big role in the development of the church in a society that didn't always esteem women, Phoebe had to be amazing. She had to be of utmost standing and she had to be a real servant leader. The first to do anything is always critiqued heavily. Can't you see her, standing straight up, filled with God's spirit and confident in Paul's recommendation? She must have caught the attention of all of the believers in Rome as she stood up to read the inspirational epistle penned by her mentor and friend, Paul. *Who is this woman?* ran through the minds of all gathered in the home of an early Christian. The fact that she was the first woman anyone had seen in leadership soon didn't matter as she stood up to speak. Her warm smile and serious commitment to the gospel caught their attention almost immediately.

My dear sisters and brothers in Christ, I am so happy to be here with you. Paul talks about you a lot. He loves you. Because you have accepted the way of Christ, I love you too. We are brothers and sisters because of our relationship with Christ. Paul would love to be with you today, but he felt compelled to visit the church at Corinth. As you already know, we are busy sharing the gospel with people throughout Jerusalem and beyond, as Christ ordered us to do. Paul has a big heart for all people who decided to follow Christ, and he wants to share all that he has learned after his encounter with the Lord. But Paul is just one man, a powerful man who is being used so mightily by God. So Paul has selected a few of us to help him with the amazing task of setting up churches. I am one of those servants. I am eager and honored to share what Paul has shared with me about Christ and share with you what I have learned on my journey. I know you may be surprised to see a woman deliver the message from Paul, but I'm here. I came today to tell you about Christ and his amazing and unconditional love. It's the message I deliver. Do not get caught up in petty things like gender and miss out on this message. I'm going to share the good news with everyone who will listen. When Paul needed someone to deliver his letter to you, dear friends, I said, send me. I packed up my bags, kissed my family good-bye, and set out on this journey to bring you the letter. It's my calling; I've got to follow it. I will remain here until Paul or another church leader can get here and be by your side. I want to answer any questions you may have and, more important, help you in any way possible as you continue on your journey to live a Christ-centered life. I know this is new for you, and I want to be right here with you as you learn more about the Way. I am here to serve you, my brothers and sisters.

I wonder what the little girls thought when they saw this sister stand up to speak, how the women felt when they saw a leader handpicked by the apostle Paul. Did they stand up straighter themselves, or did they murmur, *Why does she get to speak to us? What does she know that we don't know?*

I hope they supported this woman. I pray they listened more intently to her, knowing that she had to be outstanding to be selected in a male-dominated culture to deliver such an important message. I hope they didn't let her gender sidetrack them from hearing the importance of the message. The letter to the Romans is among the most theologically important books for Christians. It explains in detail sin and death, salvation, grace, faith, righteousness, justification, sanctification, redemption, resurrection, and glorification. Heavy-hitting theology. But once you understand it and, more important, embody it, you're transformed. You're closer to looking like Christ.

Do you carry your torch high whether you are the first, second, or last? Can those you serve *see* your values, not just hear you recite them? Do you live out the vision statement you've set forth for your organization? If you say you value work-life balance, can your community see that in you? Or do they expect you to say one thing and do the other thing? If you say you are running a ministry that cares for people, do you show that in how you care for your family and staff and others? If you say you value diversity, does your list of friends and staff reflect that you care about diversity, from the support staff through the executive ranks and board of directors?

Serving is more than creating a vision and telling people how to get there. It's more than inspiring through great words and speeches. The best visions are played out in the actions of the leader. The quickest way to get people to turn a deaf ear to your words is to live a different story. No one likes a hypocrite, and everyone can spot hypocritical rhetoric. When you say one thing and do another thing, it discredits you as a leader and makes it harder for people to believe you or follow you.

My youth minister's voice mail message included this quote from James Baldwin: "Children have never been very good at listening to their elders, but they have never failed to imitate them." It applies to leaders and those they serve too. Embody your vision and watch your community join in. Live the words you preach and watch others draw closer and closer to you to get a better view of Christ.

Can your team see Christ in your every move, or just when you're talking about Christ? Can your team understand the vision without the vision statement because they see you embodying it? Can your mate or children share your values because they have seen you live them out, not just speak about them?

Be a Working Leader

Paul could have sent this important letter by a regular courier, but he chose Phoebe specifically. He even asked the people to take really good care of her. Why? Because he knew she'd be serving them, pouring out her heart for them, and physically using her hands to work for them and minister to their needs. She was not just going to read the letter; she was going to get down and dirty and do the work that was needed at the time. Are you in the trenches digging with your team, like Phoebe did as soon as she read the letter, or merely giving instructions on how to get things done?

I learned a valuable lesson while serving as a team leader at one of my jobs. My role was to make sure the work got done well. I had a team working on ancillary products for a textbook. We had to read through each chapter of a book and coordinate other items that needed to be associated with the chapters. I split the work up among the team, and I took a few chapters too. I think the team was surprised that I would actually do "work" too, but I thought it would help to get the job done faster. As I worked on my chapters, I noticed several inconsistencies. I was able to address them immediately and give better direction to the team on how to handle the issues. My manager didn't expect me to, but I'm glad I did. First, I learned as my team learned—and true leaders never stop learning. I also was able to identify with the work better because I knew firsthand what each person was dealing with. And I'm sure I gained the respect of my team. I was asking them to work hard and do some pretty tedious work, and I was doing some of it too. And I was showing—not just talking about—my commitment to get the work done.

I was first struck by this *working-leader model* at my first full-time job at a children's publication. Each week, a new paper had to be written and designed. On our team, we had two editor-writers and an art director. The editors explained the issue to the art director in a weekly meeting, and the art director worked with researchers to find photographs and illustrators to create illustrations. Well, at one meeting, I noticed that the art director's manager was there and was working as the designer, taking notes for the upcoming issue. Because I was young and new and looked for every opportunity to grow at that stage (oh, for the zeal of youth to remain with us even as we mature), I asked her why she was designing this particular issue. She said she volunteered to design one issue for each of her staff members, particularly when they seemed overwhelmed or had other projects to complete. "I like to design, and this way I still can, and I get to help my team when they are stressed."

Point well received. Some managers are all about giving the orders, making the meetings, setting the agendas, and making sure their workers are doing their jobs, while others are about teamwork, setting the vision, and helping get the job done with elbow grease.

Do others see you chipping in? Do they see you treating members of your household with respect or just barking out orders? Do you model your vision and work ethic while at home, at work, and in the community or just state it?

There's nothing more eye-opening or satisfying than to sit with your people and catch a view from their level. It's one of the reasons I like the show *Undercover Boss*. The leaders of companies go undercover and take on jobs that may seem menial but honestly are the heart of the company—movers, factory workers, and so on. They get to see how the work really gets done. Have you sat down and listened to those you lead? What are their concerns? They certainly may be different than your concerns.

Anyone who has taken a writing class has heard the phrase *show, don't tell*. Stories, illustrations, and examples make the point much better than a declarative statement. Likewise, our actions show our values and our vision much more than our words do. Show, don't tell. Live it out, don't just declare it. What letter do you need to deliver to those around you? Do it through your actions.

———

Dear God, make me a model of your service. Help me to live a life that shows others you and your grace. Give me the wisdom and grace to lead through my actions, not just my words. I desire to be a living letter for you. Give me strength as I run this race for you, seeking to serve you through service to your people. Amen.

Live your mission more than you speak it.

Peter

Successful leaders are strong and
faith-filled.

Now I say to you that you are Peter (which means
'rock'), and upon this rock I will build my church,
and all the powers of hell will not conquer it.

(Matthew 16:18, NLT)

Successful leaders understand the need to embody
strength and still remain human and vulnerable
to those around them. When I took an unscientific
Facebook poll of my friends about the qualities they
admire in leaders, not one person said they like a
wimpy and uncertain leader. No one wants to follow
a leader who doesn't have confidence in her vision or
one who doesn't display that confidence. A tentative
leader will be dismissed quickly. People want to follow

someone they can believe in, someone they believe can take their organization to another level, the place in their vision. People need a strong leader. And the only way to be a strong Christian leader is to have strong faith in the Christ you follow.

One of the strongest people in the scriptures is Peter—so much so that he is even called a rock. That single word alone sounds strong. *Rock* sounds solid. The word conjures up visions of our modern-day poster child for strength: Dwayne Johnson (also known as The Rock). His chiseled body represents strength. His roles in movies represent safety as he rescues kids or families or a damsel in distress. Peter may not have looked like Dwayne Johnson—or maybe he did, lifting all of those fish from the water—but Peter is called a rock from the mouth of Jesus. The King of Kings proclaimed that Peter was a rock.

Rocks are strong. Rocks are solid, and while they do break, it takes a great force to break them because rocks are formed over time. Some are formed when molten lava cools and settles. It takes time to be rock hard and solid. It takes heat and pressure and the cooling-off process to make you strong and rocklike.

Rocks can also be formed when bits and pieces of soil and other parts of Earth's surface settle upon each other. Over time they too develop into rock-hard pieces, not easily broken. They've already been through so much pressure that it takes a tremendous amount of pressure to break sedimentary rocks. Time, experience. Life. Heat. Trials and tribulations make leaders solid and strong and rocklike.

Marble, a precious and expensive rock used in beautiful homes and structures, is formed when limestone is subjected to heat and pressure. More precious, more beautiful solid rock forms after some additional heat and pressure occur.

The best rocks emerge after some real knockout fights and battles. Those battles don't leave a successful leader forever scarred; they leave you stronger and more dependent on Christ, the true solid rock. A successful leader recognizes that he's been through the battle. She relies on the same person she knows got her through that battle to get her through the next one. As she cools down from the battles of life, a certain peace settles over her, making her faith rock solid but her heart even more attuned to the grace and mercy that comes from a relationship with Christ. It's a rough process that turns out beautifully, strong and solid (see Romans 8:28 and Philippians 4:7).

Some who go through trials and tribulations just get hard. They are not helpful or visionary or hopeful. They are the opposite: hard and unbreakable and unbendable. The hard stuff in life has made them cynical and bitter. Only their hearts have been hardened against dreaming and living and expecting. That's not the type of leader Peter was. No, Peter was more like Christ, the solid rock we stand on. Peter was named the rock because of his belief in Christ.

Look at how Peter gets this, in Matthew 16:16. Peter boldly declares that Christ is the Messiah, the one who has come to save us from our sins; as evidenced by the answers of the others in previous verses, not everyone understood Christ's purpose. But Peter got it. Peter declared who Jesus was in this section in Matthew, and because of his understanding of the Messiah, Peter was called the rock. Christ himself declared that the church would be built upon the rock, Peter. Peter would go on to play a significant role in building the church. His rock-solid leadership would benefit the early church and even those of today.

But like rock, Peter, I believe, underwent a process to become solid and faith-filled.

Rock in Formation

To become solid in our faith and in our leadership, we need to be students. In order to have faith in what Christ can do, we need to know Christ. Peter was a student of Christ. He was one of the chosen twelve who followed Jesus around for at least three years of Jesus' ministry on Earth. Peter was by Jesus' side. Do you consider yourself a student of Jesus (or do you think you've learned it all)?

Peter asked questions. He wasn't merely a follower of Christ soaking up all the goodness of walking side by side with the Messiah. No, he took advantage of his close and personal relationship with Christ. He pondered this new way of thinking that Christ was showing him, and he asked the questions, even if others may have thought they were silly questions. Can't you hear him wondering about this forgiveness concept Christ is preaching about? He asks Jesus in Matthew 18:21: *So exactly how much do I need to implement this forgiveness thing? You know, some people just keep doing wrong. How long should I give them to do it? Seven times—that seems like enough, right, Jesus?* From his questions, he learned even more, especially when our Savior reminded Peter that we should forgive much more than seven times. In fact, the model teacher showed how to forgive over and over again. Peter learned because Peter was bold enough and sincere enough and willing enough to ask the questions. How many questions do you ask God? Do you spend time searching scriptures when a thought arises in your head, or do you turn elsewhere first for your answer? To build rock-solid faith, seek answers from God. Peter was loud and bold. Even when your questions seem dumb or simple, be bold enough to seek out Bible-believing, faith-filled mentors to discuss your thoughts with. One of my favorite friends is a theologically trained questioner of God. She always has questions about God. I love her faith and her boldness to inquire. Even though she is a church leader, she still asks questions. We don't always come up with the answers, but we normally leave our conversations strengthened and enlightened.

And from questions come understanding, and rock-solid faith is formed. Even with his trials and tribulations (denying Christ, not once or twice, but three times, when things got too hot [Matthew 26:69–75]), acting rashly when he was angry (John 18:10), or falling asleep when Jesus himself had specifically asked him to pray (Mark 14:32–42), Peter was named the rock; he was entrusted with the vision and the keys to heaven (Matthew 16:19). He was not perfect, yet he was a rock-solid successful leader. God is not looking for the perfect leader, but the one who is ready and willing to be formed by Christ's example.

Peter didn't change his personality just because he was called by God. He was fiery. My pastor often calls him a thug. (He did show up with a knife and cut a man! See John 18:10.) He spoke up and out—often loud and out of order (John 13:7–9). Leadership doesn't change who you are naturally; you may be shaped and molded to be more like Christ, but your personality will show through. Peter's fieriness showed up even as he followed Christ. He carried his personality with him because he was an authentic leader. He wasn't trying to be someone he was not. He was comfortable in his skin, and therefore he was able to become comfortable with Christ. If you are unable to be vulnerable with your Lord, how in the world will you be a vulnerable leader, one showing that you are as human as the next person, just transformed by your faith in Christ?

No Room for Pretense

Peter was not a pretender; he brought his entire being to Christ and followed wholeheartedly. Look at him when Jesus let him preview what was to come (Matthew 17:1–13), the glory and the suffering. Jesus took Peter, along with James and John, to a mountaintop. On the mountain, Jesus was transfigured, and these three disciples got to experience firsthand the divine side of Christ. No longer was he just a man walking among them; he was Lord. He was God Almighty; they saw his divine state, not his human body. And then, almost as if bearing witness to the divinity of Christ, heroes of the faith Moses and Elijah appeared and talked with Jesus. This amazing visit had to be a glimpse of glory to come, where the people we've read about and heard about for their great faith and leadership convene. When he was allowed to glimpse glory, to be in the presence of those great leaders, Peter told Jesus: "Lord, it is good for us to be here, if you wish, I will put up three shelters—one for you, one for Moses and one for Elijah" (Matthew 17:4). Peter was so enthralled and caught up in this indescribable moment in time that he wanted to stay right there. Peter wanted to set up camp and make it comfortable for his heroes. I can hear him: *Jesus is Lord! I knew this man was special. I just knew you were the Son of the Living God. I said it. I believed it. You confirmed it for me, but this... this is too much. You are God. You, the one I've been walking with and talking with and serving with. You are God. James and John, he is the One. And look who our God and Lord is talking with. The amazing leader Moses—the one who God handpicked to deliver the Israelites from Egypt. The man who confirmed the special relationship God had with his people and told them how to live. And right there next to Moses is Elijah, who did so many amazing things, all in the name of our God. He wanted the people to follow the one and only living God, and he stood up to those evil kings, the ones who wanted the people to worship their gods. This is so good, I don't think we should go anywhere. I want to stay right here forever. I want to be in the presence of these great leaders always!*

Peter was in the presence of God and the great leaders of his faith, struck with childlike awe. He couldn't act cool and calm. He couldn't act like this was a regular encounter. No, when you realize who Christ really is you throw out protocol and become

a starstruck child. You desire to stay in the presence
of such power and greatness forever. Peter's reaction
shows that he acknowledged that he was witnessing
greatness and wanted to stay around it forever.

Leader, when you encounter those special God
moments, the times when you know it was nothing but God who made something happen, throw
caution to the wind and celebrate. You may shout,
you may sit and say a silent prayer, you may sing a
tune, but you know that when you stumble across
greatness, you can't be cool and calm. You can't pre-
tend that this is ordinary. A strong leader can still
get giddy about the extraordinary. A strong leader
can still rejoice with glee when something amazing
happens. It shows others that your belief is not in
your skills or your tasks but in God. It shows others
that you can still be surprised by God. Yes, I've got
a vision; yes, I've got a plan; but I follow God, and
sometimes God takes me off of that plan and takes
me to a mountain and does something out of the
ordinary. And when that happens, I can't act like it
is a regular day.

When was the last time your family saw you act out
of order because Christ has done something amazing
in your life? When was the last time your team was

called in for a special celebration and you let them know things went extraordinarily well, and you're pleased and excited and want them to keep on doing what they've been doing? Solid leaders know how to celebrate. Rock-hard folks know when it's time to rejoice and break up the day with a little extra party: it's not an ordinary day, and I can't act like it is.

Peter also has yet another noteworthy characteristic of a successful leader: his ability to do the unthinkable. Just like he broke protocol and called for a special building fund just to keep Jesus, Elijah, and Moses on that mountaintop, Peter also wanted to walk on water when he saw Jesus out in the water. Peter hadn't stopped to think how impossible this is; he just wanted to do it if Jesus was doing it. He wanted to be where Jesus was and he wanted to do what Jesus did. Even though Peter had been walking with Jesus and witnessing all he had done, Peter was still amazed by Jesus. (Leaders don't stop getting amazed by Jesus, no matter how long we've walked beside him.) So when Jesus came walking toward their boat, walking on water, and told his disciples not to be afraid, Peter proclaimed: *All right then, if it is you Lord, let me walk with you.*

Jesus then simply said: *All right. Come on, Peter.*

And just like that Peter did the unthinkable. Peter defied the laws of gravity and walked on water. Some people focus on the fact that he didn't walk long; he began to look around and become amazed at what was really happening. He was walking on water! And that made him lose focus on Jesus, who was allowing him to defy natural laws.

Leader, stay focused on the miracle worker, not the miracles. I don't want to dwell on what made Peter fall. I want to dwell on what made Peter walk. It was his faith in Jesus. He knew Jesus was God; he had already proclaimed it. He knew Jesus could do anything; he had already seen it. So he was acting upon his faith. And while preparation is important and planning is vital, sometimes what empowers a successful leader do the impossible is simply trusting. A successful leader knows faith is the key. A successful leader knows that some things can go awry even when all of the formulas are correct. That doesn't trip you up; you keep plugging away, you keep trusting. And likewise, a successful leader recognizes that sometimes you've got to jump and do what looks foolish. Not because you're leading by irrational emotions, but because you are trusting in a God that some can't understand—a God even you can't always understand—but you believe. You trust. You've seen him walk on water. You've seen him perform miracles. You've got to jump out of the boat and do the bold thing. Do the unthinkable. Not because you're Superman or Superwoman, but because you know who can do the impossible.

—

Jesus, my Lord, I declare that you are the Holy One with all power. I am your follower. I am your child. I am still in awe of you. Strengthen my faith each day so that I may do the things that seem impossible, not because of my efforts, but because of your grace and strength. I know I can do all things through you and only through you, for you strengthen me. I love you. I am in awe of your goodness, power, and love. Never let me lose focus. Never let me get trapped in the ordinary. I want to remain in awe of you. I want to do the impossible.

Develop stronger faith as you become a strong leader.

Paul

Successful leaders are passionate.

...though I myself have reason for confidence in the flesh also. If anyone else thinks he has reason for confidence in the flesh, I have more: circumcised on the eighth day, of the people of Israel, of the tribe of Benjamin, a Hebrew of Hebrews; as to the law, a Pharisee; as to zeal, a persecutor of the church; as to righteousness under the law, blameless. But whatever gain I had, I counted as loss for the sake of Christ. Indeed, I count everything as loss because of the surpassing worth of knowing Christ Jesus my Lord. For his sake I have suffered the loss of all things and count them as rubbish, in order that I may gain Christ...

(Philippians 3:4–8, ESV)

Theologian Howard Thurman says, "Don't ask what the world needs. Ask what makes you come alive, and go do it. Because what the world needs is people who have come alive." Yet finding what makes you come alive, what your passion is, isn't always intuitive. We don't always understand how our inclinations can fit into a calling, or a job, or a sustainable lifelong career. We don't always easily recognize what we are good at doing or what we could do without caring how much time we spent on it. We choose careers based on what our parents expected, what we thought we liked to do (although we normally haven't even lived much of our lives when we're asked to choose), or what we thought paid well, or sometimes we chose simply from what was available to us at the time we needed a job. Our hobbies are sometimes based on what our parents could afford (or desired) to have us do as young kids when we had so much more time to develop and take classes and spend hours upon hours playing an instrument or decorating a jar or practicing a sport.

But how does an adult, one burdened with responsibilities, bills, loans, and all of the stuff of life, become alive to the passions within and turn them into a tangible skill that not only takes care of our needs but also helps others? It's a tough question successful leaders ponder as well as exemplify. When you see a leader working in his or her passion area, you see a successful leader. When you see someone doing exactly what they were purposed to do, whether they knew it on day one or discovered it in year fifty, you see a successful leader. She can inspire. He can give his all and develop others. Because once you've discovered the feeling of being alive and operating in your passion area to fulfill your purpose, you can't keep the secret to yourself. You want others to feel the same way and follow their calling, and a successful leader desires to help them develop into all they are destined to become.

This type of passion and this type of calling is seen in the apostle Paul, the writer of most of the letters in the New Testament that shape and inform our faith.

I admit to having a love-hate relationship with Paul and his writings. Still, my favorite scriptures are from books ascribed to Paul. I sometimes dislike Paul, for the same reason Thurman's grandmother told him not to read those letters to her, to just focus on the words of Jesus in the New Testament. Some of Paul's words have been used to support slavery, suppress women, and create havoc in the church.

Yet notwithstanding the critiques, Paul leads as he writes, even while imprisoned. This leader of the new church was resilient, passionate, and fully dedicated to his causes. Paul embodies passion. He lives it, he writes it, he shares it, he makes others want to follow his lead and live passionately.

Fiery Passion

Paul's passion is easily recognized even from the first time we see this man in scripture (Acts 8:1); he was named Saul then and was present at the stoning of the apostle Stephen. We see Saul standing right there at Stephen's death, giving approval to the death of a man who was preaching about Christ. Saul was a leader even at this time. He was a leader on the other side of Christianity—one who persecuted Christians, one who thought the Messiah would look different, one who upheld the Jewish laws at the time. Even when he was on the wrong side of the fence, Saul was a leader. He demonstrated fiery passion and followed through on his convictions. He thought Christians were wrong and crazy, and he did what he could to stop them from spreading their message.

A leader stands by his or her convictions to the end. And she shows up during the fight! Leadership is not about giving orders and commanding those around us to do the dirty work. True leaders show up, especially when it matters. People believe in leaders who believe in what they are doing and saying. Saul believed the church should be stopped. Saul believed Stephen should be stoned, and he was right there as the rocks were being hurled. Even on the wrong side, Saul was displaying leadership qualities.

But God used that fiery passion for the church rather than against the church. Oh, that we all could transfer our passion for worldly things—sports, our children, our hobbies—and use them for God's kingdom. When Saul was busy doing what he did best, trying to stop the growth of the church (Acts 9:1–2), God got his attention. It's noteworthy to say that even as a leader on the opposite side, Saul knew the importance of following protocol. He didn't just haphazardly run off and persecute Christians. He got letters from the high priest giving him permission and authority to arrest anyone preaching about Jesus. He followed protocol because passion doesn't prevent you from following procedures. A rally can't become effective if it has no organization. A protest is subject to become a riot if the attendees refuse to follow rules. Passion doesn't dismiss order, regardless of how fiery it is.

So when Saul was on his way to Damascus with letters ready to persecute, God decided to redirect his amazing passion. Saul got a personal visit from Jesus, who spoke directly to him. Saul was stopped in his tracks. As he fell to the ground, he heard the Lord's voice: *Saul, Saul, why do you persecute me?*

At this point, Saul recognized that something was going amiss. He asked, "Who are you, Lord?" (already recognizing that he was in the presence of God). *I am Jesus, whom you are persecuting. Now, get up and go into the city and you will be told what you must do.*

Just like that—after his encounter with the Lord—Saul gets up and does what he is told to do. Thankfully, a follower of Christ, Ananias, was faithful to God and did as he was instructed, although I'm sure everyone around him thought he was crazy. Ananias had been called to restore Saul's sight (literally and spiritually) and tell him more about Jesus, whom he had just encountered. Ananias was called upon to be bold and do the unthinkable: evangelize to the man who could imprison him, witness to the one who had demonstrated hate for his message, preach to the one who had already done damage to Christians.

Leading those who look like us and think like us can often be easier than doing the bold and unknown thing. Even when we feel a push and a prod from God, it takes an exceptional person to do the unthinkable, to give our all to the one who has already bitten us. But thankfully, Ananias listened to God and believed God's promise to make Paul an "instrument" to carry his name throughout the world (Acts 9:15).

Paul's conversion was implemented. He spent time studying and talking with the Christians, now that he had been called to the other side. He got his training to be a successful leader to Christians and those God was calling to become Christians. And God used his preaching abilities and writing abilities for good. His words were amazing. His writing was impassioned. But his real testimony was the way he lived. People were astonished to see his change. He probably brought more people to Christ because they were curious. *Now, what happened to this man? Isn't this the one who was preaching against Christ and killing people who followed Jesus? What happened? I've got to go see for myself.*

It is unpopular for leaders to be too vulnerable and reveal their past struggles, but Paul couldn't hide his. The people knew. True leaders are vulnerable and share who they are. People want to follow someone they can trust and believe in, and sharing where you have come from, sharing how God helped you overcome some struggles and issues and is still helping you do this, can make others trust you. People want to hear about your life and your stories. When you tell me what happened to you, I lean in just a bit more to hear you.

Paul's life was an open book for his contemporaries as it is for us today. He went through some tough stuff as he tried to spread the Good News. He was imprisoned several times. Yet the letters he wrote while in prison are some of the most powerful and impactful scriptures. In Romans he shared the main themes of the gospel: salvation and righteousness for all humankind. He told of the awesomeness of Christ's love, which believers cannot be separated from. In Corinthians he instructed the early Christians (and even us today) how to handle conflicts and follow Christ. In Galatians he refuted legalistic living and exhorted readers to live freely by God's spirit.

Ephesians encourages believers to go deeper into the understanding of God's purpose and grace. Colossians refutes heresy and proclaims Christ as Lord.

Paul continued throughout his writings in the New Testament to proclaim Christ through his own trials and tribulations.

Renewed and Revived

The change that occurred in Paul was evident. His words were powerful and strong and his life demonstrated transformation. The once egotistical man was now a humble servant, working tirelessly to share the goodness of God with others. Even when he listed his credentials, he acknowledged that his couldn't be compared to the greatness of Christ. That marks a true leader, one who has worked hard and established good credentials but in the end knows that those really don't compare to the ultimate service and sacrifice of Christ.

His letters speak loud and clear about the man and leader he was.

My dear friends, I want you to live the best you can

live, not for yourself but for Christ, who has died just for you. I want you to understand who Christ is and all Christ has done for you. Not because of your own righteousness, but to make you right with God. I want you to forget about the things you've obtained—they've been given to you by God anyway—but I want you to focus on God and what God has done through Christ. And then I want you to use this realization to inform every aspect of your life: how you treat yourself, how you treat your mate, how you treat your kids, and even how you treat those who work for you. Truly knowing Christ changes you, it transforms you. Knowing Christ makes you think about Christ and think about others. Knowing Christ keeps you focused on God's power, not your own. Oh, what a life you have to live when you are renewed and transformed. And this is just the beginning. Wait until you see what God has planned for you in the end, when we shall all be changed and be taken to live forever with him. What a glorious day it will be. Until then, watch and wait and work not for yourself, but for Christ, as I strive to do even when I am in prison. You see, it doesn't matter where you are; you can do something for God. Your location doesn't determine your attitude. You can find a way to get a message out. You can find a way to be a leader from the prison, from your home, from the hardest places in life. If you allow God's Word to transform you, you can live out your purpose on purpose. Do it now, my friend. Live for Christ.

— ⁓ —

Gracious and Holy God, I desire to serve you from wherever I find myself. Give me the strength to focus on you to renew and transform my mind. Teach me to think about the things you have done for me through Christ so I may serve you better, so I may serve your people better. Ignite my passion so I may run on until the end, giving you all the glory. Amen.

Come alive today.

Jesus

Our model of successful leadership.

> "I am the light of the world. Whoever follows me
> will never walk in darkness, but will have the light
> of life."
>
> (John 8:12, NIV)

Jesus is our ultimate example. He is our true leader.
He became human to show us the way to live while
on this earth and to sacrifice his life for us to gain
ours. No book can possibly share all of the ways
Jesus exemplified successful leadership.

Jesus was bold. He said what needed to be said without mincing words. Whether it was challenging the
pious religious leaders of the day, demons, or his followers, Jesus spoke the truth and was unapologetic about
it (Matthew 21:12–13). Successful leaders say and do

the bold things. They stand up for what is right and refuse to let wrong go unchecked. They are fair and just and will not tolerate anything less from themselves or from those they lead. All leaders need to be fearless and bold enough to confront people and circumstances that do not support the mission and goals of the community, team, church, family, or organization.

Jesus was compassionate. Throughout the gospels, we see Jesus displaying compassion for the people he is trying to teach. He saw that they were hungry, and he provided for them (Mark 8:2). He saw that they were lost and wandering without true leadership (Mark 6:34), so he taught them. A leader can confront wrongdoing and at the same time be filled with compassion for those who are wayward, hungry, lost, oppressed, and so on. Our humanity should make our hearts ache for those who are not walking in their purpose or living up to their potential or who are searching in all the wrong places for satisfaction. We should be like Jesus and have compassion—not just a feeling of pity or empathy, but a compassion that compels us to help in any way we can. In an organization, we can offer training for the one who needs help. In a church, we can offer counseling or be a mentor to the one who is struggling. At home, we can give extra support to the one who needs more attention. When our hearts are aligned with Jesus, we understand that successful leadership serves people. Have we worked to meet their needs? Has compassion led us to care for them and guide them? If we're following Jesus, our master example, we will be filled with compassion.

Jesus was connected to God. As the Son of God, divinity clothed in humanity, Jesus couldn't get disconnected from God. He was God. Likewise, successful leaders need to be intimately connected with God at all times. We need to be like branches attached to the vine (John 15), recognizing that we cannot move or function or be our true selves if we are not attached to our vine, our maker and power source. Constant daily prayer, fellowship with believers, Bible study, time spent thinking about all of God's deeds can keep us in connection with God. We can never get too busy to stop and commune with God; it will make us powerless quickly. A successful leader desires to grow closer to God each day, knowing we can't have too much of God. As we come nearer and nearer to our Lord, the Bible says God will draw closer to us (James 4:8).

Jesus asked for help and accepted it. While traveling throughout Jerusalem and surrounding areas,

Jesus often needed help. He needed to be fed (his physical body got hungry), he needed places to rest his head, and he needed companions. When Martha prepared a meal, he ate it. When the women traveling with him supported his mission financially, he accepted their graciousness. Successful leaders understand that they cannot complete their mission alone, even if it feels like it would be easier that way. No one can do it alone. While we need God's strength and help, we also need the help of people around us. Christ-like leaders know how to say yes to help, realizing that it will mean empowering others to do a job in their own way. We give up micromanaging and control to allow others to help us meet our mission and our goal. We joyfully and willingly allow others the opportunity to use their gifts to meet our common goals. *Help* is not a bad word; it is Christ-like.

Jesus relaxed and had downtime with God and others. Several passages in scripture show Jesus enjoying time away with his friends, even if some people wondered what in the world he was doing eating with sinners. (Everyone he met was a sinner.) Jesus was serious about his mission; the most serious mission of all time was and is salvation. However, Jesus had time to just sit and enjoy himself with his friends. He was not always on the grind. Sometimes we need to sit down and rejuvenate, and that comes from enjoying time with those who want little from us or from those who can actually serve us and care for our needs. When was the last time you truly enjoyed yourself with your loved ones without being distracted by the e-mails popping up on your phone or without reading through reports and other work? Do you take vacations, dedicated time away from the mission to just relax? Do you regularly observe Sabbath rest, a time to stop and recognize that the world will not stop spinning if you are not at work? Jesus did.

Jesus was not a celebrity. Jesus didn't aspire to make headlines, and neither should successful leaders. When your mission is serving God, you recognize that some people will love you, and in just one minute, those same people can despise you. Your eyes shouldn't be set on people and their opinions of you. Serving is not a popularity contest. Witnessing and sharing the gospel of Christ is not making friends or getting fans. Jesus had all of that and didn't let it get to him. He was much smarter and wiser than that. He understood the human condition. He understood that people would praise you one second and crucify you the next. He stayed focused on his goals and his mission, and we all benefit because he did. Regardless of what level of popularity you attain as a successful leader, follow Jesus' example and don't reduce your God-given mission to a popularity contest.

Jesus healed. Through his words, through his teachings, through his encounters with others, Jesus was all about setting demons free and helping people be whole and alive and free. Let your words bring healing and not harm. Let your presence make people better, not worse. Model Jesus' ability to make people their best. Only through prayer can we do these things (Mark 9:29). Stay prayerful as you touch others' lives.

Jesus got sad and overwhelmed. In Mark 16:34–36, we are reminded that Jesus really did walk among us as a human. He had human emotions. And one of those emotions was sadness, because of the overwhelming sacrifice of his mission. When faced with the cross and his ultimate mission—death for the sins of the world—Jesus had a moment where he wanted out. It can be hard to realize yet liberating at the same time. Jesus was "overwhelmed with sorrow." Yet what he does next is the example we are to follow. He cried out to God. He admitted his feelings and took them to the One who could help. Successful leaders are able to function with their emotions, not suppressing them or allowing them to overrule them. We know how to deal with the myriad emotions that can crop up as we work toward our mission. Denying our emotions can lead to depression, uncontrollable anger, bitterness, misplaced aggression, and so much more. When we find ourselves overtaken with an emotion, we can be like Jesus. Recognize that emotion. Name that emotion. And find the prayer closet where you can have a little talk with our Lord. That's where you can find fuel to carry on just as Jesus did when he emerged from prayer saying, "Yet not what I will, but what you will." That's the true declaration of a servant's heart.

Jesus walked with his enemies near his side. The ugly truth is that not everyone is for you. You can try your best and do your best, but in the end, some people will not want to support your mission or your cause. You just can't do anything about those people. Jesus walked with the one who betrayed him. Jesus knew who would give him up (Mark 14:20–21) and betray him. However, Jesus didn't allow Judas' façade of friendship to stop him or distract him. Jesus was still able to operate and walk toward his mission with Judas by his side. In fact, Judas' betrayal played right into Jesus' mission. So instead of focusing on those who are not really with you, keep focusing on your mission. Don't spend your energy worrying about them and their antics.

Jesus gives us so many other examples of successful leadership—too many to list in one volume. But the successful leader recognizes the boundless amount of inspiration, guidance, and instructions buried in God's Word awaiting our discovery. Successful leaders commit to learning more and more about God as they grow each day. Our life reflects lifetime learning; our faith walk reflects lifetime growth in Christ. As we strive to live out our God-given mission, we strive to live nearer and nearer to our God. For without our Lord, we can do nothing. But with God, we know and believe, all things are possible (Matthew 19:26). So, with our minds fixed on our mission, we march on. With our spirits connected to God, humbly awaiting our direction, we seek to lead like Christ, knowing our success comes only from God.

My Lord and my God, I commit my service to you. I want to do your will for my life. I want to be a leader like Christ: humble, mission-filled, compassionate, helpful, and whole. Make me look more and more like Christ each day. Through your spirit and through your strength alone. Amen.

Live like Jesus every day.

Acknowledgments

I appreciate all of the help I've had in bringing this book to light. The team at Hachette is always great to work with; we're on book number three and I appreciate you even more: Adrienne Ingrum, Grace Tweedy, Carolyn Kurek, Bob Castillo, Melissa Mathlin, and Jody Waldrup.

I'm grateful to my husband, Derrick, and my daughter, Kayla, for patiently allowing me the time to write. I'm also very thankful to all of the leaders who have helped shape my thoughts shared in this book. My mom and dad (Mr. and Mrs. Manuel Washington) were the first leaders I observed, and they served as great role models.

And as always, I'm thankful to God for allowing me to study the Word and to write to inspire others. I pray these words will help you to press on in faith.